ICELAND: A TRAVEL GUIDE

ZION HALLEL

All rights reserved. No part of this publication may be reproduced, distributed, or transmitted in any form or by any means, including photocopying, recording, or other electronic or mechanical methods, without the prior written permission of the publisher, except in the case of brief quotations embodied in critical reviews and certain other noncommercial uses permitted by copyright law.

Copyright © (ZION HALLEL) (2023).

TABLE OF CONTENTS

INTRODUCTION — 7

CHAPTER 1 — 9
- Location and Geography — 9
- Climate and Weather — 11
- Brief History and Culture — 14
- Practical Information — 17

CHAPTER 2. Planning Your Trip — 21
- Best Time to Visit — 21
- Duration of Stay — 23
- Entry Requirements and Visa Information — 25
- Getting to Iceland — 27
- Transportation within Iceland — 30
- Accommodation Options — 33

CHAPTER 3. Reykjavik: The Capital City — 37
- Overview of Reykjavik — 37
- Top Attractions and Landmarks — 40
- Museums and Cultural Sites — 43
- Shopping and Dining — 46
- Nightlife and Entertainment — 49

CHAPTER 4. Exploring the Golden Circle — 53
- Thingvellir National Park — 53
- Geysir Geothermal Area — 55
- Gullfoss Waterfall — 58
- Other Highlights in the Golden Circle — 60

CHAPTER 5. The Majestic South Coast — 65
- Seljalandsfoss Waterfall — 65
- Skogafoss Waterfall — 67
- Black Sand Beaches — 70

Jokulsarlon Glacier Lagoon	72
Vatnajokull National Park	75

CHAPTER 6. Discovering the Stunning Westfjords — 79

Introduction to the Westfjords	79
Dynjandi Waterfall	81
Hornstrandir Nature Reserve	83
Látrabjarg Cliff	86
Remote Villages and Local Culture	88

CHAPTER 7. The Magical Northern Lights — 93

Understanding the Northern Lights	93
Best Time and Locations for Viewing	95
Photography Tips and Techniques	98

CHAPTER 8. Outdoor Adventures and Activities — 103

Hiking and Trekking	103
Glacier Tours and Ice Climbing	105
Whale Watching	108
Hot Springs and Geothermal Baths	110
Horseback Riding and Bird Watching	112

CHAPTER 9. Wildlife and Nature Reserves — 117

Snaefellsnes Peninsula	117
Lake Myvatn and the Dimmuborgir Lava Fields	119
Puffin Colonies	122
Arctic Foxes and Reindeer	125

CHAPTER 10. Off the Beaten Path — 129

Remote Highlands	129
Westman Islands	132
Askja Caldera	134

    Thorsmork Nature Reserve   137
    Vestmannaeyjar Archipelago   139

CHAPTER 11. Practical Tips and Advice   **143**
    Safety and Health Information   143
    Money and Currency Exchange   146
    Communication and Internet Access   148
    Packing Essentials   151
    Local Etiquette and Customs   154

CHAPTER 12. Icelandic Cuisine and Local Delicacies   **157**
    Traditional Icelandic Dishes   157
    Seafood Specialties   159
    Unique Ingredients and Flavours   162
    Recommended Restaurants and Cafes   165

CHAPTER 13. Language and Useful Phrases   **169**
    Basic Icelandic Phrases   169
    English Proficiency in Iceland   170
    Language Learning Resources   172

CHAPTER 14. Additional Resources   **177**
    Recommended Books and Travel Guides   177
    Online Travel   179

INTRODUCTION

Welcome to the land of fire and ice, where otherworldly landscapes and enchanting natural wonders await your discovery. Welcome to Iceland, a place where geothermal energy powers the spirit of adventure and where ancient sagas meet modern innovation. From towering glaciers to cascading waterfalls, rugged lava fields to steaming hot springs, this Nordic island nation offers a sensory feast like no other. Prepare to embark on a journey of awe-inspiring beauty and unforgettable experiences as we unveil the wonders of Iceland through this comprehensive travel guide. Whether you're seeking thrilling outdoor adventures, a glimpse into rich Viking heritage, or simply a moment of tranquility amidst breathtaking landscapes, Iceland has it all. So pack your bags, don your warmest layers, and let us be your guide to an extraordinary Icelandic adventure. Get ready to immerse yourself in the land of sagas, where nature reigns supreme and the unexpected awaits at every turn. Welcome to Iceland, where dreams become reality.

CHAPTER 1

Location and Geography

Iceland, located in the North Atlantic Ocean, is a Nordic island country known for its stunning landscapes, geothermal activity, and unique geological features. It is situated at the junction of the North American and Eurasian tectonic plates, which has shaped its dramatic terrain and resulted in a high level of volcanic and geothermal activity.

Geographically, Iceland is located between Greenland and Norway, with a latitude range of approximately 63° to 67° N and a longitude range of about 13° to 24° W. The country is relatively small in size, covering an area of around 103,000 square kilometres (40,000 square miles), making it the most sparsely populated country in Europe.

Iceland's terrain is characterized by diverse landscapes, including volcanoes, glaciers, hot springs, geysers, lava fields, and fjords. The interior of the country is largely uninhabited and features rugged mountains, vast lava deserts, and sand plains known as "sands" or "deserts." Some of the notable mountains in Iceland include Hvannadalshnúkur, which is the highest peak in the country, and Eyjafjallajökull, famous for its 2010 eruption that caused air travel disruptions.

Glaciers cover about 11% of Iceland's land area, including Vatnajökull, the largest glacier in Europe. These glaciers give rise to numerous glacial rivers, which carve deep valleys and create magnificent waterfalls such as Gullfoss and Seljalandsfoss. The country also boasts several geothermal areas, such as the famous Geysir geothermal field, where the original geyser from which all others are named, Geysir, is located.

In terms of human settlements, the majority of Iceland's population resides along the coastline, particularly in the capital city of Reykjavik and the surrounding urban areas. Reykjavik is the northernmost capital city in the world and serves as the economic, cultural, and political center of the country.

Due to its high latitude, Iceland experiences significant seasonal variations in daylight. In summer, the "Midnight Sun" phenomenon occurs, where the sun remains visible for the majority of the day, while in winter, the country experiences long nights and shorter daylight hours.

Overall, Iceland's unique location and geography contribute to its distinctiveness and make it a popular destination for nature lovers, adventure seekers, and those interested in geology and natural phenomena.

Climate and Weather

Iceland is known for its unique climate and weather patterns, largely influenced by its location in the North Atlantic Ocean. The island's location near the Arctic Circle and the meeting point of warm and cold ocean currents creates a cool, maritime climate with relatively mild winters and cool summers. However, Iceland's weather can be quite changeable and unpredictable, and it is often said that one can experience all four seasons in a single day.

Here are some key aspects of the climate and weather in Iceland:

1. Temperatures: Iceland generally has a cool climate throughout the year. The average temperature in winter ranges from around -1°C to 4°C (30°F to 39°F), while in summer, temperatures typically range from 10°C to 15°C (50°F to 59°F).

Coastal areas are usually milder than inland regions.

2. Precipitation: Iceland receives a significant amount of precipitation, primarily in the form of rain or snow. The south and southwest coasts tend to be wetter compared to the northern and northeastern regions. The precipitation is often influenced by low-pressure systems coming from the North Atlantic, leading to frequent rainfall and cloudy skies.

3. Wind: Iceland is known for its strong winds, which can be quite powerful, especially during the winter months. These winds are influenced by the contrast between the cold Arctic air and the relatively warmer ocean currents. Wind speeds can vary greatly across the country and can have a significant impact on the weather conditions.

4. Daylight and darkness: Iceland experiences significant variations in daylight hours throughout the year due to its high latitude. During the summer months, especially around the summer solstice in late June, Iceland experiences the phenomenon known as the Midnight Sun, where the sun remains visible for almost 24 hours a day. Conversely, during the winter, particularly around the winter

solstice in late December, Iceland experiences long periods of darkness, with only a few hours of daylight.

5. Volatility: One notable characteristic of Iceland's weather is its volatility. The weather can change rapidly, and it is not uncommon to experience multiple weather conditions in a single day. Sunny skies can quickly turn into rain or snow showers, and vice versa. This variability is attributed to the influence of the North Atlantic Ocean and the meeting of different air masses.

6. Glaciers and ice caps: Iceland is home to several glaciers and ice caps, including Vatnajökull, Europe's largest ice cap. These ice formations play a crucial role in the country's climate and weather patterns. Glacial meltwater feeds into rivers and creates unique landscapes, and the glaciers themselves can influence local weather conditions.

It's important to note that climate and weather patterns can vary across different regions of Iceland. Coastal areas, for instance, tend to have milder and more moderate weather compared to the inland highlands. Additionally, Iceland's climate is subject to long-term changes and influences from global climate patterns, such as the

North Atlantic Oscillation and the Arctic Oscillation, which can impact its weather on a larger scale.

Brief History and Culture

Iceland, a Nordic island nation located in the North Atlantic Ocean, has a rich history and unique culture that spans over a millennium. Let's explore a brief overview of Iceland's history and delve into its vibrant cultural heritage.

History:
The settlement of Iceland is believed to have begun in the late 9th century when Norse explorers, led by Ingólfr Arnarson, established the first permanent settlement at Reykjavík in 874 AD. These settlers were primarily of Norse and Celtic origin, bringing with them their languages, traditions, and social structures.

During the next few centuries, Iceland developed as an independent commonwealth, governed by the Alþingi, an open-air assembly of chieftains and their followers. However, in the 13th century, conflicts and power struggles led to the loss of independence. In 1262, Iceland came under

Norwegian rule, and later in 1380, it became a part of the Kalmar Union, under Danish control.

Danish rule lasted for centuries, characterised by economic hardships, natural disasters, and restrictions on Icelandic trade. Iceland's struggle for independence began in the 19th century, gaining momentum in the early 20th century. In 1918, Iceland became a sovereign state under the Danish crown, and in 1944, it finally achieved full independence as the Republic of Iceland.

Culture:
Icelandic culture is rooted in its historical and natural surroundings, as well as the country's isolation from the rest of Europe. Here are some key aspects of Icelandic culture:

1. Language: The Icelandic language is a descendant of Old Norse and has changed relatively little over the centuries. Icelandic people take pride in their language and strive to preserve its purity, making it one of the most unchanged languages in the world.

2. Literature: Iceland has a strong literary tradition, dating back to the mediaeval sagas. These sagas are epic narratives that recount the historical and mythological events of the early Icelandic

settlers. Notable Icelandic authors include Snorri Sturluson, Halldór Laxness, and more recently, Sjón and Arnaldur Indriðason.

3. Music and Art: Icelandic music has gained international recognition in recent years, with artists like Björk, Sigur Rós, and Of Monsters and Men making a global impact. The country also hosts numerous music festivals, showcasing a diverse range of genres. Icelandic art is often inspired by the country's landscapes and folklore.

4. Nature and Outdoor Activities: Iceland's dramatic landscapes, including volcanoes, geysers, glaciers, and waterfalls, are an integral part of its culture. Outdoor activities like hiking, horse riding, and exploring hot springs are popular among locals and tourists alike.

5. Cuisine: Traditional Icelandic cuisine is centred around the island's natural resources, including fish, lamb, and dairy products. Unique dishes like hákarl (fermented shark), skyr (a type of yoghurt), and Icelandic-style hot dogs are notable culinary offerings.

6. Modern Society: Iceland is known for its progressive and egalitarian society. It was one of

the first countries to grant women the right to vote and has been a pioneer in gender equality. The country also places a strong emphasis on environmental sustainability and renewable energy.

Iceland's history and culture are deeply intertwined, shaping the identity of its people and providing a distinct and fascinating experience for visitors to the country. From its ancient sagas to its stunning landscapes, Iceland continues to captivate and inspire people around the world.

Practical Information

Iceland is a beautiful country known for its stunning landscapes, unique geological features, and vibrant culture. Here are some practical information and tips for visiting Iceland:

1. Weather: Iceland has a temperate maritime climate, but it can be quite unpredictable. Be prepared for sudden changes in weather, including rain, wind, and even snow, no matter the time of year. Layered clothing and waterproof outerwear are essential.

2. Currency: The currency used in Iceland is the Icelandic Krona (ISK). Credit and debit cards are

widely accepted, but it's a good idea to have some cash for smaller establishments and rural areas.

3. Language: The official language of Iceland is Icelandic, but English is widely spoken and understood, especially in tourist areas. You should have no trouble communicating in English.

4. Transportation: Public transportation in Iceland is limited outside of major cities. Renting a car is the most popular and practical way to explore the country. Driving conditions can vary, so be cautious, follow traffic rules, and check road conditions before embarking on a journey.

5. Accommodation: Iceland offers a range of accommodation options, including hotels, guesthouses, hostels, and campsites. It's advisable to book in advance, especially during peak tourist seasons.

6. Food and Water: Icelandic cuisine often features fish, lamb, dairy products, and local specialties like fermented shark and dried fish. Tap water in Iceland is safe to drink and of excellent quality.

7. Safety: Iceland is considered a safe country with low crime rates. However, always take standard

precautions to safeguard your belongings and valuables.

8. Natural Wonders: Iceland is famous for its natural wonders, such as waterfalls, geysers, hot springs, glaciers, and volcanic landscapes. Be sure to visit popular attractions like the Blue Lagoon, Gullfoss waterfall, Geysir geothermal area, and the Jökulsárlón glacier lagoon.

9. Outdoor Activities: Iceland is a haven for outdoor enthusiasts. Hiking, glacier walks, ice climbing, whale watching, horseback riding, and exploring lava caves are just a few of the activities available. Remember to follow safety guidelines and use experienced guides for activities like glacier hikes.

10. Midnight Sun and Northern Lights: In summer, Iceland experiences the midnight sun, where the sun can be visible even at midnight. This phenomenon offers extended daylight hours for exploration. During winter, the northern lights (Aurora Borealis) can be seen in clear, dark skies, away from light pollution.

Remember to check the latest travel advisories and regulations before your trip, as conditions and requirements can change. Enjoy your visit to

Iceland and take in the incredible beauty it has to offer!

CHAPTER 2. Planning Your Trip

Best Time to Visit

Iceland is a stunning country with diverse landscapes, geothermal wonders, and unique natural phenomena. The best time to visit Iceland depends on your interests and the experiences you are seeking. Here's a breakdown of the different seasons and what they offer:

1. Summer (June to August): The summer months are the most popular time to visit Iceland. The weather is relatively mild, with temperatures ranging from 10°C to 20°C (50°F to 68°F). During this time, you can enjoy the midnight sun, as the days are long and bright. The highland roads and hiking trails are accessible, making it an ideal time for outdoor activities like hiking, camping, and exploring the countryside. Summer is also a great time for birdwatching and visiting Iceland's numerous waterfalls and scenic locations.

2. Shoulder Seasons (May and September): The shoulder seasons can be a fantastic time to visit Iceland. In May, you can witness the arrival of

spring, with vibrant green landscapes and the possibility of catching the Northern Lights (though they are less frequent than in winter). In September, you can experience the stunning autumn foliage and enjoy fewer crowds compared to the summer months. The weather can be unpredictable, with occasional rain and cooler temperatures, but it's still possible to explore the outdoors and partake in activities like hiking and glacier tours.

3. Winter (October to April): Winter in Iceland is known for its unique and magical experiences. From October to April, you have a chance to witness the Northern Lights, especially during the darker months of December and January. The weather can be cold, with temperatures ranging from -5°C to 5°C (23°F to 41°F), but it provides opportunities for activities like ice cave exploration, snowmobiling, and soaking in geothermal hot springs. It's important to note that some highland roads may be closed during winter, limiting access to certain areas.

Ultimately, the best time to visit Iceland depends on your preferences. If you're interested in long daylight hours, outdoor adventures, and a vibrant atmosphere, summer is a great choice. If you prefer fewer crowds, stunning landscapes, and the chance to see the Northern Lights, the shoulder seasons and winter can be equally rewarding. Just remember to check the weather forecast and road conditions before planning any activities, as Icelandic weather can be unpredictable year-round.

Duration of Stay

Iceland is a captivating country known for its breathtaking landscapes, geothermal wonders, and vibrant culture. When it comes to the duration of stay in Iceland, it largely depends on your personal preferences, available time, and the experiences you wish to have. Here are a few factors to consider:

1. Short Visits: If you have limited time or are on a tight schedule, a short visit to Iceland can still offer you a taste of its unique attractions. A duration of 3 to 5 days can allow you to explore Reykjavik, the capital city, take a tour along the Golden Circle to witness geysers, waterfalls, and the Thingvellir National Park, and even indulge in a relaxing dip in the famous Blue Lagoon.

2. Week-Long Adventure: To delve deeper into Iceland's natural wonders, a week-long stay can be ideal. In addition to the Golden Circle, you can

explore the South Coast with its stunning waterfalls, black sand beaches, and glaciers. Consider visiting Jokulsarlon, the glacial lagoon, and nearby Vatnajokull National Park for a truly immersive experience. You may also have the opportunity to explore the Snæfellsnes Peninsula, known for its diverse landscapes.

3. Extended Exploration: For a more comprehensive exploration of Iceland's diverse regions, consider a stay of two weeks or longer. This allows you to venture beyond the popular tourist spots and discover lesser-known areas. You can explore the remote Westfjords, visit the stunning Eastfjords, or embark on a multi-day trek in the Highlands, which are only accessible during the summer months.

Moreover, the duration of your stay may also be influenced by your interests. If you are passionate about photography, outdoor activities like hiking or glacier climbing, or chasing the mesmerising Northern Lights during winter, you might want to allocate more time to accommodate those experiences.

Remember to plan your itinerary carefully, considering travel distances, weather conditions, and the specific attractions you wish to visit. Iceland's natural beauty is vast and diverse, so the longer you stay, the more you'll be able to immerse yourself in its wonders.

Entry Requirements and Visa Information

Iceland is a popular tourist destination known for its stunning natural landscapes, geothermal wonders, and vibrant culture. If you're planning a visit to Iceland, it's essential to understand the entry requirements and visa information before you travel. Here's an overview of what you need to know:

1. Visa Requirements:
  - Visa-Free Entry: Citizens of the European Union (EU), European Economic Area (EEA), and Schengen Area countries can enter Iceland without a visa and stay for up to 90 days within a 180-day period.
  - Visa-Exempt Countries: Citizens of several countries outside the EU/EEA/Schengen Area, including the United States, Canada, Australia, New Zealand, and Japan, can visit Iceland for up to 90 days without a visa. It's important to check the

Icelandic Directorate of Immigration website for an updated list of visa-exempt countries.
   - Visa-Required Countries: Visitors from countries not covered by the visa exemption agreements must apply for a Schengen visa through the appropriate Icelandic embassy or consulate in their home country.

2. Valid Passport:
   - All travellers, regardless of their nationality, must possess a valid passport to enter Iceland.
   - The passport should be valid for at least three months beyond the intended departure date from Iceland.

3. COVID-19 Considerations:
   - Due to the global COVID-19 pandemic, additional travel restrictions and health requirements may be in place. It's crucial to stay updated on the latest travel advisories and entry regulations before planning your trip to Iceland.

4. Visa Extensions:
   - If you wish to extend your stay beyond the allowed 90 days, you must apply for a residence permit or visa extension from the Icelandic Directorate of Immigration before your initial visa expires.

5. Work and Study Permits:
   - If you plan to work or study in Iceland, additional permits and visas may be required. It's best to consult the Icelandic Directorate of Immigration or the Icelandic embassy/consulate in your home country for detailed information on work and study visa requirements.

It's important to note that entry requirements and visa information can change over time. Therefore, it's advisable to check the official website of the Icelandic Directorate of Immigration or contact the nearest Icelandic embassy/consulate for the most accurate and up-to-date information before your trip.

Getting to Iceland

Getting to Iceland is an exciting journey that takes you to a unique and stunning destination. Iceland is a Nordic island country located in the North Atlantic Ocean, known for its dramatic landscapes, geothermal hot springs, glaciers, and volcanoes. If you're planning a trip to Iceland, here's some information on how to get there.

By Air:
The most common way to reach Iceland is by air. Keflavík International Airport (KEF) is Iceland's primary international gateway, situated about 50 kilometres southwest of the capital city, Reykjavík. Many major airlines operate direct flights to Keflavík Airport from various cities around the world. Flying to Iceland is often the fastest and most convenient option, especially for international travellers.

By Sea:
If you're looking for a different experience, you can also consider reaching Iceland by sea. Several cruise lines offer itineraries that include Iceland, allowing you to enjoy a more leisurely journey while enjoying the breathtaking coastal views. Reykjavík and Akureyri are the main ports of call for cruise ships.

Within Iceland:
Once you arrive in Iceland, you'll have several options for getting around the country.

1. Rental Cars: Renting a car is a popular choice among travellers as it offers the flexibility to explore Iceland at your own pace. You can rent a car at the airport or in Reykjavík, and Iceland has a

well-developed road network, including the famous Ring Road that encircles the island.

2. Public Transportation: Iceland has a public bus system that connects major towns and cities, but it may not be as comprehensive or frequent as in other countries. Buses are a viable option if you're travelling on a budget, but they may have limited schedules, especially in remote areas.

3. Guided Tours: Joining guided tours is a great way to explore Iceland's highlights, especially if you prefer not to drive yourself. Various tour companies offer day trips and multi-day tours to popular attractions, such as the Golden Circle, the South Coast, and the famous Blue Lagoon.

4. Domestic Flights: If you're planning to visit more remote regions of Iceland, such as the Westfjords or the Eastfjords, taking a domestic flight can save you time and make your journey more convenient.

It's worth noting that Iceland's weather can be unpredictable, and road conditions can vary, especially during winter. It's essential to check the weather forecast and road conditions before embarking on any journey.

Before travelling to Iceland, make sure to research and plan your itinerary based on your interests and the time you have available. Iceland offers an incredible range of natural wonders, including waterfalls, geysers, black sand beaches, and the mesmerising Northern Lights. So, prepare yourself for an unforgettable adventure in this captivating land of fire and ice.

Transportation within Iceland

Transportation within Iceland primarily relies on road networks, with a few additional options available. The country has a well-developed road system that provides access to various destinations, including major cities, towns, and popular tourist attractions. Here are some key aspects of transportation within Iceland:

1. Car Rental: Renting a car is a popular choice for exploring Iceland. Reykjavik, the capital city, has several car rental agencies, and there are additional options at Keflavik International Airport. Renting a car provides the flexibility to travel at your own pace, discover remote areas, and enjoy Iceland's scenic landscapes. It's important to note that during winter, driving conditions can be challenging, so it's

recommended to choose a suitable vehicle and check the weather and road conditions regularly.

2. Public Transportation: Iceland has a public bus system operated by Strætó. The bus routes primarily cover the Reykjavik metropolitan area and nearby towns. Public transportation services are more limited in rural areas, so it's advisable to plan your trip accordingly. The bus network does provide transportation to some popular tourist destinations, such as the Golden Circle and the Blue Lagoon.

3. Domestic Flights: If you're looking to travel between different regions of Iceland quickly, domestic flights are available. Air Iceland Connect operates flights from Reykjavik to several destinations across the country. Flying can be convenient when visiting places like Akureyri, the Westfjords, or the Eastfjords, especially if you have limited time.

4. Ferries: Iceland has a few ferry services that operate between certain towns and islands. For example, the Baldur ferry connects Stykkishólmur on the Snæfellsnes Peninsula with the Westfjords, and the Herjólfur ferry links the mainland with the Westman Islands. These ferries provide an

alternative means of transportation and are particularly useful for exploring remote coastal areas.

5. Taxis and Ride-Sharing: Taxis are available in Reykjavik and other major towns. Ride-sharing services like Uber and Lyft do not currently operate in Iceland, but local taxi companies provide similar services. Taxis are generally more expensive than other modes of transportation, so it's advisable to inquire about fares beforehand.

6. Cycling and Walking: Iceland's cities and towns are generally pedestrian-friendly, and walking is an excellent way to explore urban areas. Cycling is also an option in some places, and bike rentals are available in Reykjavik. However, it's important to note that Iceland's challenging weather and long distances between certain attractions might make cycling a more suitable choice for experienced cyclists or shorter distances.

It's worth mentioning that Iceland's rugged and diverse landscapes often require careful planning and consideration for safety. It's recommended to check road conditions, weather forecasts, and travel alerts before embarking on any journey within Iceland.

Accommodation Options

Iceland is a popular tourist destination known for its stunning natural landscapes, geothermal wonders, and vibrant culture. When it comes to accommodation options, Iceland offers a range of choices to suit different budgets and preferences. Here are some of the common accommodation options available in Iceland:

1. Hotels: Iceland has a variety of hotels ranging from luxury establishments to budget-friendly options. In major cities like Reykjavik, you'll find internationally recognized hotel chains as well as boutique hotels offering comfortable rooms, amenities, and often stunning views of the surrounding landscapes.

2. Guesthouses: Guesthouses are a popular choice in Iceland, especially in rural areas. These are typically smaller, family-run establishments that provide a cosy and homely atmosphere. Guesthouses often offer comfortable rooms with shared or private bathrooms, communal living spaces, and home-cooked meals. Staying in a guesthouse is a great way to experience Icelandic hospitality and get insights from locals.

3. Farm Stays: Iceland's rural areas are dotted with working farms that offer accommodation options known as farm stays. These provide a unique opportunity to experience the country's agricultural lifestyle. Guests can stay in farm houses or cottages, participate in farm activities, and enjoy fresh local produce. Farm stays are ideal for those seeking a more authentic and immersive experience.

4. Hostels: Hostels are an affordable choice for budget-conscious travellers. They offer dormitory-style accommodations with shared facilities such as kitchens and common areas. Hostels are a great way to meet fellow travellers and often provide communal activities and tours. Reykjavik has several hostels, while some are also found in other popular tourist destinations.

5. Camping: Iceland's breathtaking natural beauty makes it a haven for outdoor enthusiasts, and camping is a popular option for those seeking an adventurous experience. The country has numerous well-equipped campsites, some with facilities like showers, toilets, and cooking areas. However, it's important to note that wild camping is prohibited in many areas, so make sure to check the regulations and use designated campsites.

6. Holiday Rentals: Another popular option, especially for families or larger groups, is to rent holiday homes or cabins. These are often fully furnished and equipped with amenities like kitchens and private bathrooms. Holiday rentals can be found throughout Iceland, both in cities and rural areas, and offer more space and privacy compared to hotels or guesthouses.

It's worth noting that Iceland can be a popular tourist destination, especially during the peak summer season, so it's advisable to book your accommodation well in advance. Additionally, prices may vary depending on the time of year, location, and the type of accommodation you choose.

Whether you prefer luxury hotels, cosy guesthouses, or immersive farm stays, Iceland offers a range of accommodation options to suit different tastes and budgets, ensuring a memorable stay surrounded by the country's breathtaking landscapes.

CHAPTER 3. Reykjavik: The Capital City

Overview of Reykjavik

Reykjavik is the capital and largest city of Iceland, located on the southwestern coast of the island. It is known for its stunning natural landscapes, vibrant cultural scene, and unique blend of modernity and traditional charm. As the economic, political, and cultural centre of Iceland, Reykjavik offers a range of attractions and activities for visitors to enjoy.

One of the remarkable features of Reykjavik is its picturesque setting. The city is surrounded by breathtaking natural beauty, with the Atlantic Ocean to the west and majestic mountains to the north. The nearby presence of glaciers, geysers, and hot springs adds to the city's allure, making it a gateway to Iceland's exceptional natural wonders.

Reykjavik has a compact and walkable city centre, allowing visitors to explore its many attractions on foot. The heart of the city is characterised by colourful, low-rise buildings, modern architecture, and wide, tree-lined streets. Laugavegur, the main shopping street, is bustling with boutiques, restaurants, cafes, and art galleries, offering a vibrant and lively atmosphere.

The city is home to several iconic landmarks. One of the most famous is Hallgrímskirkja, a stunning Lutheran church and the tallest building in Iceland. Its unique design, inspired by the basalt columns found in Iceland's nature, provides visitors with panoramic views of the city from its observation deck.

Another must-visit attraction is the Harpa Concert Hall and Conference Center, an architectural marvel featuring a distinctive glass facade. Harpa hosts various cultural events, including concerts, exhibitions, and conferences, and it has become a symbol of Reykjavik's modernity and artistic spirit.

Reykjavik is also known for its vibrant cultural scene. The city is brimming with art galleries, museums, theatres, and music venues, showcasing Iceland's rich artistic heritage. The National Museum of Iceland offers insights into the country's history and culture, while the Reykjavik Art Museum displays a diverse collection of contemporary and modern art.

The city's nightlife is lively and renowned. Reykjavik has a thriving music scene with a wide range of live music venues, from intimate cafes to larger concert halls. The city's bars and clubs cater to diverse tastes, offering everything from cosy pubs to trendy nightspots.

Reykjavik's proximity to nature allows visitors to engage in a variety of outdoor activities. Popular excursions include exploring the Golden Circle, which includes the geothermal area of Geysir, the breathtaking Gullfoss waterfall, and the historic Þingvellir National Park. Visitors can also enjoy whale watching tours, horseback riding, glacier hikes, and relaxing in geothermal spas such as the Blue Lagoon.

In terms of culinary experiences, Reykjavik has a thriving food scene with a focus on fresh, local ingredients. Visitors can savour Icelandic delicacies like lamb, seafood, and skyr (traditional Icelandic yoghourt). The city is also known for its vibrant café culture, with numerous cosy coffee shops offering a warm and welcoming atmosphere.

Overall, Reykjavik offers a unique blend of natural wonders, cultural attractions, and a modern urban environment. Its combination of stunning landscapes, vibrant arts scene, and warm hospitality make it an unforgettable destination for travellers from around the world.

Top Attractions and Landmarks

Iceland is a breathtaking country known for its dramatic landscapes, volcanoes, geothermal activity, and stunning natural beauty. Here are some of the top attractions and landmarks that make Iceland a unique and must-visit destination:

1. The Golden Circle: The Golden Circle is a popular tourist route that includes three primary sites: Þingvellir National Park, the Geysir geothermal area, and the Gullfoss waterfall. Þingvellir National Park is a UNESCO World Heritage Site and holds historical significance as the location of Iceland's first parliament. The Geysir geothermal area is home to the famous Strokkur geyser, which erupts regularly, and Gullfoss is a majestic two-tiered waterfall.

2. Blue Lagoon: Located in a lava field on the Reykjanes Peninsula, the Blue Lagoon is a geothermal spa that offers a unique and relaxing experience. The milky-blue, mineral-rich waters are rich in silica and are known for their healing

properties. Visitors can enjoy bathing in the warm waters while surrounded by the rugged Icelandic landscape.

3. Jökulsárlón Glacier Lagoon: Situated in southeast Iceland, Jökulsárlón is a stunning glacial lake filled with icebergs that have calved off the nearby Breiðamerkurjökull glacier. The turquoise waters and floating icebergs create a mesmerising sight. Boat tours are available to get a closer look at the icebergs and the nearby Diamond Beach, where icebergs wash up on the black volcanic sand.

4. Dettifoss: Known as Europe's most powerful waterfall, Dettifoss is located in Vatnajökull National Park in northeast Iceland. The sheer volume and force of water cascading down the rugged cliffs create a thunderous spectacle. The surrounding landscape, with its basalt formations and dramatic canyons, adds to the beauty of this natural wonder.

5. Reykjavik: Iceland's capital city, Reykjavik, offers a vibrant mix of culture, history, and modern attractions. Explore the colourful buildings in the old town, visit the iconic Hallgrimskirkja church, and immerse yourself in the city's thriving arts and music scene. The Harpa Concert Hall and the Sun

Voyager sculpture are also notable landmarks worth visiting.

6. Seljalandsfoss: This picturesque waterfall is one of Iceland's most famous. What sets it apart is the ability to walk behind the waterfall curtain, offering a unique perspective and incredible photo opportunities. Nearby, you'll also find the equally beautiful Skógafoss waterfall, which is larger in size and equally impressive.

7. Skaftafell Nature Reserve: Located within Vatnajökull National Park, Skaftafell offers a diverse range of landscapes, including glaciers, ice caves, mountains, and lush green valleys. It's a paradise for hikers and nature enthusiasts, with numerous trails leading to breathtaking viewpoints and natural wonders.

8. Landmannalaugar: Nestled in the highlands of Iceland, Landmannalaugar is known for its colourful rhyolite mountains, hot springs, and stunning hiking trails. The area is a popular starting point for the Laugavegur hiking trail, which takes you through some of Iceland's most awe-inspiring landscapes.

These are just a few of the many attractions and landmarks that Iceland has to offer. Whether you're captivated by waterfalls, geothermal wonders, glaciers, or unique geological formations, Iceland's natural beauty is sure to leave you in awe.

Museums and Cultural Sites

Iceland is a country known for its stunning natural landscapes, but it also has a rich cultural heritage showcased through its museums and cultural sites. From historical artefacts to contemporary art, there are several notable museums and cultural sites in Iceland that offer visitors a deeper understanding of the country's history, art, and culture. Here are a few worth exploring:

1. The National Museum of Iceland (Þjóðminjasafn): Located in Reykjavík, the National Museum provides a comprehensive overview of Iceland's history, from the settlement era to modern times. The museum houses a diverse collection of artefacts, including archaeological finds, mediaeval manuscripts, traditional costumes, and historical documents.

2. The Saga Museum (Saga-Múseet): Situated in Reykjavík, the Saga Museum takes visitors on a

journey through Iceland's sagas, which are mediaeval narratives of the country's early settlers and heroes. The museum features life-size wax figures and captivating exhibits that bring these sagas to life.

3. The Reykjavík Art Museum (Listasafn Reykjavíkur): This museum comprises three separate locations: Hafnarhús, Kjarvalsstaðir, and Ásmundarsafn. Each venue offers a unique art experience, showcasing both Icelandic and international works. The museum focuses on contemporary and modern art, hosting exhibitions, installations, and events throughout the year.

4. The Settlement Exhibition (Landnámssýningin): Located in Reykjavík, this museum is built around an archaeological excavation site that reveals the remains of a Viking Age longhouse. Through interactive displays and multimedia presentations, visitors can learn about the lives of early settlers in Iceland.

5. The National Gallery of Iceland (Listasafn Íslands): Situated in Reykjavík, the National Gallery houses a vast collection of Icelandic visual art from the 19th century to the present day. The museum

features a variety of mediums, including painting, sculpture, photography, and video art.

6. The Icelandic Phallological Museum (Hið íslenzka reðasafn): Located in Reykjavík, this unique museum is dedicated to the study and display of penises from various mammals found in Iceland and around the world. It offers a quirky and unconventional perspective on anatomy and culture.

7. The Vatnajökull Visitor Center (Hof) and Jökulsárlón Glacier Lagoon: Situated in southeast Iceland, this visitor centre provides information about the Vatnajökull glacier, Europe's largest glacier. Visitors can learn about glacial processes, climate change, and the unique ecosystem surrounding the glacier. The nearby Jökulsárlón Glacier Lagoon offers breathtaking views of icebergs floating in a glacial lake.

8. The Snorrastofa Cultural and Medieval Centre: Located in Reykholt, this cultural centre is dedicated to the mediaeval Icelandic writer and historian Snorri Sturluson. It offers insights into the life and works of Snorri, who wrote the famous Prose Edda, a significant source of Norse mythology.

These are just a few examples of the museums and cultural sites you can explore in Iceland. Whether you're interested in history, art, or natural wonders, Iceland's cultural offerings provide a unique and enriching experience for visitors.

Shopping and Dining

Shopping and dining in Iceland offer unique and delightful experiences for visitors. Whether you're exploring the vibrant city of Reykjavik or venturing into the smaller towns and villages, you'll find a variety of options to satisfy your shopping cravings and culinary desires.

Shopping in Iceland:

1. Reykjavik: The capital city is a shopaholic's paradise, with a blend of international brands, local designers, and specialty stores. Laugavegur is the main shopping street, lined with fashion boutiques, art galleries, and souvenir shops. You can find Icelandic wool products, handmade crafts, jewelry, and artwork that reflect the country's culture and heritage.

2. Kolaportið Flea Market: Located near Reykjavik's harbour, this indoor flea market is a treasure trove for unique finds. Here, you can browse through vintage clothing, books, antiques, vinyl records, and Icelandic delicacies. It's a great place to immerse yourself in the local culture and pick up some one-of-a-kind souvenirs.

3. Handknitting Association of Iceland: For those interested in traditional Icelandic wool products, a visit to this association is a must. You can find beautifully hand-knit sweaters, hats, scarves, and other woollen items made by local artisans. The quality and craftsmanship of these products are exceptional.

4. Farmers' Markets: Throughout Iceland, you'll find farmers' markets where you can purchase fresh produce, locally made food products, and unique culinary delights. The markets provide an excellent opportunity to taste traditional Icelandic dishes, such as fermented shark, smoked fish, and various dairy products.

Dining in Iceland:

1. Icelandic Cuisine: Icelandic cuisine is influenced by the country's geographical location and natural

resources. Traditional dishes often feature fish, lamb, dairy products, and local ingredients like seaweed and berries. Popular dishes include "Plokkfiskur" (mashed fish with potatoes), "Hangikjöt" (smoked lamb), and "Skyr" (a thick yoghourt-like dairy product).

2. Seafood: Iceland's proximity to the North Atlantic Ocean ensures an abundance of fresh seafood. Restaurants serve a wide range of fish and seafood delicacies, including langoustine (Icelandic lobster), salmon, cod, and arctic char. You can enjoy these dishes in various preparations, from grilled to smoked to pan-fried.

3. Reykjavik Restaurants: Reykjavik boasts a vibrant culinary scene, offering a diverse range of international cuisines alongside traditional Icelandic fare. From fine dining establishments to casual bistros and cosy cafes, there's something for every palate. You can explore Nordic cuisine, fusion dishes, sushi, burgers, and much more.

4. Geothermal Cuisine: Iceland's geothermal activity allows for unique culinary experiences. For example, some restaurants offer the opportunity to dine in geothermal greenhouses where you can

enjoy meals prepared with ingredients grown using geothermal heat.

5. Icelandic Craft Beer: Beer enthusiasts will find a growing craft beer scene in Iceland. Microbreweries have gained popularity, and you can sample a variety of local brews, including those infused with Icelandic herbs and flavours.

It's worth noting that dining out in Iceland can be quite expensive compared to some other countries, so it's a good idea to plan your budget accordingly. Additionally, it's advisable to make reservations in advance, especially for popular restaurants in Reykjavik, to ensure you secure a table during peak tourist seasons.

Nightlife and Entertainment

Iceland may be known for its stunning natural landscapes, including glaciers, geysers, and waterfalls, but it also offers a vibrant nightlife and entertainment scene. Despite its relatively small population, Reykjavik, the capital city of Iceland, has a thriving nightlife that caters to both locals and tourists. Here's a glimpse into the nightlife and entertainment options you can find in Iceland:

1. Bars and Clubs: Reykjavik boasts a wide variety of bars and clubs that cater to different tastes and preferences. The city centre, especially the Laugavegur and Hverfisgata streets, is lined with numerous establishments offering everything from live music and DJ sets to themed parties and karaoke nights. Some popular venues include Kaffibarinn, Dillon, Paloma, and Húrra.

2. Live Music: Iceland has a rich music scene, and live music performances are a prominent part of its nightlife. You can find venues featuring a diverse range of genres, from local Icelandic bands to international acts. The iconic Harpa Concert Hall hosts various concerts throughout the year, ranging from classical music to contemporary pop and rock. Smaller venues like Gaukurinn and Húrra often showcase up-and-coming local talent and underground bands.

3. Festivals: Iceland is known for hosting several music festivals that attract visitors from around the world. The most famous is the Iceland Airwaves festival, held annually in Reykjavik. It showcases both established and emerging Icelandic and international artists across various venues in the city. Other notable festivals include Secret Solstice, which takes place during the summer solstice, and

Sónar Reykjavík, focusing on electronic and experimental music.

4. Comedy: Comedy clubs have gained popularity in Reykjavik, offering laughter-filled evenings for locals and tourists alike. These clubs feature both local and international stand-up comedians, providing entertainment through humorous performances in both Icelandic and English.

5. Cultural Events: Iceland celebrates its culture and heritage through various events and festivals throughout the year. These events showcase traditional music, dance, art, and literature, allowing visitors to experience the unique Icelandic culture firsthand. The Reykjavik Arts Festival, held annually, brings together local and international artists for a diverse range of exhibitions and performances.

6. Thermal Pools and Spas: While not strictly nightlife, thermal pools and spas play a significant role in Iceland's entertainment scene. The country is known for its geothermal activity, and Reykjavik offers several public pools and private spas where you can relax in hot springs and enjoy various wellness treatments.

It's important to note that Iceland's nightlife can be influenced by the season, with longer days and more outdoor activities available during the summer months. Additionally, some venues may have specific age restrictions or require reservations, particularly during peak tourist seasons. Therefore, it's advisable to check for event listings and plan accordingly to make the most of Iceland's nightlife and entertainment offerings.

CHAPTER 4. Exploring the Golden Circle

Thingvellir National Park

Thingvellir National Park is a magnificent natural wonder located in Iceland, renowned for its geological and historical significance. Situated approximately 40 kilometres east of the capital city of Reykjavik, Thingvellir holds immense cultural importance as the site of Iceland's ancient parliamentary assembly, the Alþingi, which convened there from 930 to 1798.

The park's geological significance stems from its location on the Mid-Atlantic Ridge, where the Eurasian and North American tectonic plates meet. This geological phenomenon makes Thingvellir a unique place to witness the visible effects of plate tectonics. The shifting of the tectonic plates has created a rift valley, characterised by dramatic cliffs and gorges, including the prominent Almannagjá gorge.

One of the most striking features of Thingvellir National Park is the Silfra Fissure. This underwater crevice is a diver's paradise, offering crystal-clear waters and unparalleled visibility. Divers can immerse themselves in the narrow fissure, which boasts astonishingly clear glacial water and the opportunity to swim between the continents.

Thingvellir also holds great significance in Icelandic history and culture. It served as the gathering place for the early Icelandic settlers who established the world's first parliament, the Alþingi, in 930 AD. The Alþingi played a crucial role in the governance and legal system of the Icelandic Commonwealth, making Thingvellir the symbolic heart of Iceland's political heritage.

In addition to its cultural and geological attractions, Thingvellir National Park is renowned for its breathtaking natural beauty. The park encompasses a diverse range of landscapes, including moss-covered lava fields, sparkling lakes, and serene forests. The picturesque Þingvallavatn Lake, the largest natural lake in Iceland, graces the park's surroundings, adding to its scenic allure.

The park offers various hiking trails, allowing visitors to explore its captivating vistas and encounter its rich flora and fauna. During summer, the park is adorned with vibrant wildflowers, while in winter, it transforms into a winter wonderland, with snow-covered landscapes that showcase Iceland's enchanting beauty.

Thingvellir National Park's outstanding universal value has been recognized by UNESCO, which designated it as a World Heritage Site in 2004. Its geological significance, historical importance, and natural splendour combine to create an awe-inspiring destination that attracts visitors from around the world.

Whether you are interested in geology, history, outdoor activities, or simply immersing yourself in Iceland's stunning landscapes, Thingvellir National Park is a must-visit destination that offers a remarkable blend of natural and cultural wonders.

Geysir Geothermal Area

Geysir Geothermal Area, located in Iceland, is one of the country's most famous tourist attractions. It is situated in the Haukadalur Valley, approximately 100 kilometres east of the capital city, Reykjavik. The geothermal area is renowned for its spectacular hot springs, geysers, and other geothermal phenomena.

The name "Geysir" actually comes from the Icelandic word for "gusher" or "erupt." The area is named after the Great Geysir, which is the oldest known geyser in Europe and one of the main attractions within the geothermal area. Although the Great Geysir is not as active as it once was, its eruptions can still reach heights of up to 70 metres, although they are infrequent.

The most active geyser in the Geysir Geothermal Area is Strokkur, which erupts every few minutes, shooting boiling water up to 30 metres into the air. This predictable and impressive display makes Strokkur a favourite among visitors. People gather around the geyser, eagerly waiting for its eruption and capturing the moment with their cameras.

Apart from Geysir and Strokkur, there are several other hot springs and geothermal features in the area. These include hot pools, steam vents, and smaller geysers. The landscape is characterised by colourful mineral deposits, bubbling mud pots, and a distinct smell of sulphur, which is common in geothermal areas.

The Geysir Geothermal Area is not only a popular tourist destination but also holds scientific significance. It offers valuable insights into geothermal activity and its geological processes. The high temperature and pressure conditions within the area are a result of Iceland's unique position on the Mid-Atlantic Ridge, a tectonic boundary between the North American and Eurasian plates.

Tourists visiting the Geysir Geothermal Area can explore the walking paths and wooden boardwalks that provide access to the various geothermal features. There are also educational exhibits and information boards explaining the geology, history, and significance of the area. Additionally, visitors can relax in the nearby hot springs or enjoy the stunning natural beauty of the surrounding landscape.

It is important to note that while the Geysir Geothermal Area is a captivating and awe-inspiring place, it is essential to adhere to safety guidelines and respect the fragile ecosystem. Visitors should stay on designated paths, avoid touching the hot springs or geysers, and follow any instructions provided by the park authorities.

In summary, the Geysir Geothermal Area in Iceland offers a unique opportunity to witness the power and beauty of geothermal activity. With its iconic geysers, hot springs, and geological wonders, it is a must-visit destination for nature lovers, geology enthusiasts, and anyone seeking an unforgettable experience in Iceland's remarkable natural landscapes.

Gullfoss Waterfall

Gullfoss Waterfall, also known as the "Golden Falls," is a magnificent natural wonder located in southwestern Iceland. It is one of the country's most iconic and popular tourist attractions, drawing visitors from all around the world. The waterfall is situated in the canyon of the Hvítá river, which originates from the Langjökull glacier.

What makes Gullfoss Waterfall truly captivating is its sheer size and dramatic beauty. The Hvítá river plunges down in two tiers, creating a stunning double cascade that drops approximately 32 metres (105 feet) into a narrow, rugged gorge. The water flows with tremendous force, creating an awe-inspiring spectacle as it crashes into the canyon below. The waterfall's thunderous roar and the mist rising from the cascading water contribute to its mesmerising atmosphere.

The name "Gullfoss" translates to "Golden Falls" in English, and it stems from the golden hue that the water takes on when the sunlight hits it on a clear day. The sun's rays reflecting off the mist and spray can create a beautiful golden shimmer, enhancing the waterfall's enchanting allure.

Gullfoss Waterfall is not only known for its natural beauty but also for its rich history. The waterfall has played a significant role in Icelandic conservation efforts. In the early 20th century, when plans were made to harness the power of the waterfall for hydroelectric purposes, a local woman named Sigríður Tómasdóttir fought tirelessly to preserve Gullfoss. Her efforts were successful, and Gullfoss was eventually protected as a national monument in 1979, ensuring its conservation for future generations to enjoy.

Visiting Gullfoss allows you to witness the raw power and grandeur of nature up close. Several viewing platforms and paths provide excellent vantage points to admire the waterfall from different angles. The experience of standing near the rushing water and feeling its spray is both exhilarating and humbling.

Gullfoss is also a popular stop along the Golden Circle route, a famous tourist trail in Iceland that includes other notable attractions such as the geothermal area of Geysir and the historic Þingvellir National Park. Many tours and excursions offer the opportunity to explore these sights together, making it a convenient and rewarding way to experience Iceland's natural wonders.

In summary, Gullfoss Waterfall in Iceland is a breathtaking natural marvel renowned for its immense beauty and historical significance. Its towering cascades, powerful flow, and the golden glow it can emanate make it a must-visit destination for nature lovers and adventure seekers alike.

Other Highlights in the Golden Circle

The Golden Circle is a popular tourist route in Iceland, known for its stunning natural landscapes and historical sites. In addition to the well-known attractions like Þingvellir National Park, Geysir geothermal area, and Gullfoss waterfall, there are several other highlights worth exploring along the Golden Circle. Here are some of them:

1. Kerið Crater: Located in the Grímsnes area, Kerið is a volcanic crater lake that offers a unique and picturesque landscape. The crater is approximately 3,000 years old and is characterised by its vibrant red volcanic rock walls and a deep blue lake at the bottom. Visitors can walk along the crater rim, descend to the water's edge, and even go inside the crater.

2. Faxi Waterfall: Often overshadowed by its famous neighbour, Gullfoss, Faxi Waterfall is a hidden gem worth visiting. Located on the Tungufljót River, Faxi offers a tranquil and serene atmosphere. The waterfall is about 80 metres wide and cascades down into a beautiful pool below. It's an excellent spot for photography and a peaceful stop along the Golden Circle route.

3. Secret Lagoon: If you're looking for a more relaxing experience, the Secret Lagoon, also known as Gamla Laugin, is a natural hot spring located in Flúðir. It is one of the oldest geothermal pools in Iceland, surrounded by steam rising from hot springs and a small erupting geyser nearby. The pool's water is rich in minerals and remains at a

pleasant temperature year-round, making it an ideal place to unwind and enjoy the peaceful surroundings.

4. Skálholt: For history enthusiasts, a visit to Skálholt is highly recommended. Skálholt was Iceland's educational and spiritual centre during the Middle Ages and served as the Episcopal see until the Reformation in the 16th century. Today, you can explore the ruins of the old cathedral, visit the modern church on the site, and learn about the historical and cultural significance of Skálholt through exhibitions and guided tours.

5. Brúarfoss: Known as the "Blue Waterfall," Brúarfoss is a hidden gem tucked away from the main tourist routes. It is located near the town of Laugarvatn and offers a breathtaking sight with its vibrant blue water flowing through a narrow gorge. The waterfall is surrounded by picturesque landscapes and offers fantastic photo opportunities for nature enthusiasts.

These are just a few of the other highlights along the Golden Circle in Iceland. Exploring these lesser-known attractions can provide a unique and enriching experience, allowing you to discover more of Iceland's natural beauty, history, and cultural heritage.

CHAPTER 5. The Majestic South Coast

Seljalandsfoss Waterfall

Seljalandsfoss Waterfall is a magnificent natural wonder located in Iceland, renowned for its breathtaking beauty and unique characteristics. It is situated along the southern coast of the country, approximately 120 kilometres (75 miles) from Reykjavik, the capital city. Seljalandsfoss is considered one of Iceland's most iconic and popular waterfalls, attracting numerous visitors throughout the year.

What sets Seljalandsfoss apart from many other waterfalls is the fact that it is possible to walk behind the cascading water curtain. This feature allows visitors to experience an awe-inspiring perspective as they witness the immense power and beauty of the falling water from a truly unique angle. The path behind the waterfall is well-maintained, making it accessible to most visitors. However, it's important to exercise caution as the rocks can be slippery and the area may be wet and muddy.

The waterfall itself is formed by the Seljalandsá River, which originates from the glacier-capped Eyjafjallajökull volcano. The river plummets down a 60-metre (197-foot) cliff, creating a spectacular cascade that captivates all who witness it. The sheer height and the thunderous sound of the water crashing into the pool below create a mesmerising and unforgettable sight.

Seljalandsfoss is particularly striking during the summer months when Iceland experiences long daylight hours. The waterfall is surrounded by lush greenery, wildflowers, and vibrant moss-covered rocks, enhancing its natural beauty. The continuous mist generated by the waterfall creates a shimmering effect, further adding to its ethereal charm.

Photographers and nature enthusiasts are drawn to Seljalandsfoss for its incredible photographic opportunities. The interplay of light, water, and the surrounding landscape offers endless possibilities for capturing stunning images. Whether it's capturing the golden hues of the midnight sun during the summer or the icy blue tones in winter, Seljalandsfoss provides a magical setting for photographers to unleash their creativity.

While Seljalandsfoss is undoubtedly a captivating sight, it is worth mentioning that it is not the only waterfall in the area. Nearby, you can also find the equally stunning Gljúfrafoss, often referred to as the "hidden waterfall." It is partially concealed by a cliff, creating a sense of mystery and adventure for those who seek it.

Visiting Seljalandsfoss is relatively straightforward, with a well-maintained parking lot and easy access from the Ring Road (Route 1). The waterfall is open to the public year-round, but it's important to check the conditions during the winter months, as the area can be icy and slippery.

In conclusion, Seljalandsfoss Waterfall is a true natural gem in Iceland, offering visitors a chance to immerse themselves in the awe-inspiring power of nature. Its accessibility and unique feature of walking behind the cascading water make it a must-see destination for travellers seeking unforgettable experiences in Iceland's stunning landscape.

Skogafoss Waterfall

Skogafoss Waterfall is one of the most iconic and magnificent natural landmarks in Iceland. Located in the southern part of the country, it is situated along the Skógá River, which originates from the Eyjafjallajökull glacier. The waterfall is known for its sheer beauty, impressive height, and powerful cascading waters.

Skogafoss stands at an impressive height of approximately 60 metres (197 feet) and has a width of about 25 metres (82 feet). Its thunderous roar and the mist created by the cascading water make for a truly awe-inspiring sight. On sunny days, rainbows often form in the mist, adding an extra touch of magic to the scene.

One of the unique features of Skogafoss is its accessibility. A well-maintained staircase leads visitors right to the base of the waterfall, providing an up-close and personal experience. This allows you to feel the immense power of the waterfall and witness its beauty from a different perspective. As you climb the stairs, you'll also get a fantastic panoramic view of the surrounding landscapes, including the lush green fields and rugged cliffs.

Skogafoss is not only a treat for the eyes but also a popular spot for photographers and nature enthusiasts. Its picturesque setting and dramatic backdrop make it a favourite subject for many artists. Additionally, the waterfall has been featured in numerous films and documentaries, contributing to its fame and recognition worldwide.

Apart from its visual appeal, Skogafoss also holds a special place in Icelandic folklore. According to legend, a treasure chest filled with gold lies hidden behind the waterfall. Locals believe that a brave and determined individual will one day find the chest. However, numerous attempts have been made to locate the treasure over the years, yet none have been successful so far.

For visitors who wish to explore beyond the waterfall, the Skógá River offers some exciting opportunities. The river is renowned for its salmon and trout fishing, attracting fishing enthusiasts from all around. Additionally, the nearby Skógasafn Museum provides insights into the history and cultural heritage of the region, making it an excellent complement to a visit to Skogafoss.

Whether you're an adventure seeker, a nature lover, or simply someone in awe of natural wonders, a visit to Skogafoss Waterfall in Iceland is an experience that will leave a lasting impression. Its grandeur, beauty, and accessibility make it a must-see destination for anyone travelling to this stunning Nordic country.

Black Sand Beaches

Iceland is renowned for its stunning natural landscapes, and one of its unique features is its black sand beaches. These captivating beaches are formed from volcanic activity and offer a dramatic contrast to the typical golden or white sandy beaches found in many other parts of the world. Let's delve into the beauty and allure of black sand beaches in Iceland.

The black sand beaches in Iceland owe their distinctive color to the country's volcanic geology. Iceland is situated on the Mid-Atlantic Ridge, where the Eurasian and North American tectonic plates meet. This geological activity has resulted in frequent volcanic eruptions throughout the island's history. When volcanic lava flows reach the ocean, they cool rapidly, shatter into tiny fragments, and eventually form the black sand found along the coast.

One of the most famous black sand beaches in Iceland is Reynisfjara, located on the southern coast near the village of Vík í Mýrdal. Reynisfjara is renowned for its striking basalt sea stacks called Reynisdrangar, rising dramatically from the Atlantic Ocean. These towering formations create a dramatic backdrop against the black sand, creating a photographer's paradise. However, it's important to note that Reynisfjara can be dangerous due to its powerful waves and strong currents, so visitors should exercise caution and adhere to safety guidelines.

Another remarkable black sand beach in Iceland is Djúpalónssandur, situated on the Snæfellsnes Peninsula. This beach offers a unique blend of black sand, pebbles, and fascinating rock formations. Djúpalónssandur is also known for its historical significance, as it was once a popular fishing village. Today, remnants of a shipwreck and rusted iron debris serve as reminders of the area's maritime past, adding to the beach's charm.

Iceland's black sand beaches are not just visually captivating but also offer opportunities for wildlife enthusiasts. Birdwatchers can spot various seabirds nesting and soaring along the coastline. Puffins, in particular, are a delight to observe with their distinctive appearance and comical behaviour.

It's worth noting that while these black sand beaches are awe-inspiring, the ocean surrounding Iceland can be unpredictable. Visitors should be cautious of sneaker waves, undertows, and other potential hazards. It's always advisable to follow safety guidelines, pay attention to warning signs, and consult local authorities or tour operators before venturing near the coastline.

Exploring Iceland's black sand beaches provides a unique and unforgettable experience. The juxtaposition of the dark sand, towering cliffs, and the relentless power of the Atlantic Ocean creates a captivating atmosphere. Whether you're a nature lover, a photographer, or simply seeking the untamed beauty of the natural world, Iceland's black sand beaches are sure to leave a lasting impression.

Jokulsarlon Glacier Lagoon

Jökulsárlón Glacier Lagoon is a stunning natural wonder located in southeastern Iceland. It is considered one of the country's most breathtaking and popular tourist attractions. The lagoon is situated at the head of the Breiðamerkurjökull glacier, which is an outlet glacier of the larger Vatnajökull ice cap.

The unique feature of Jökulsárlón is its glacial lake, which is filled with floating icebergs that have calved off the nearby glacier. The icebergs come in various shapes, sizes, and shades of blue, creating a mesmerising sight. The lagoon itself is quite deep, reaching depths of up to 250 metres (820 feet). It covers an area of about 18 square kilometres (7 square miles), making it the deepest and largest glacial lake in Iceland.

The constantly shifting icebergs in the lagoon create a dynamic and ever-changing landscape. The play of light and reflection on the icebergs, combined with the dramatic backdrop of snow-capped mountains, makes Jökulsárlón a photographer's paradise. Many visitors describe the experience as surreal and otherworldly.

Boat tours are a popular way to explore the lagoon up close. These tours allow visitors to sail among the floating icebergs, providing an immersive and intimate encounter with the glacier. It is also possible to take amphibious boat tours that allow you to venture onto both land and water.

Jökulsárlón has been featured in numerous films, including the James Bond movie "Die Another Day" and the Batman film "Batman Begins." Its ethereal beauty and remote location make it a favorite filming location for capturing the essence of the Icelandic landscape.

Adjacent to Jökulsárlón, you'll find a black sand beach known as Diamond Beach. This beach is adorned with icebergs that have washed ashore, creating a stunning contrast against the dark sand. It's a popular spot for photographers and nature lovers seeking a unique coastal experience.

While visiting Jökulsárlón, it's important to respect the natural environment and follow any guidelines provided by local authorities. The lagoon is a fragile ecosystem, and efforts are made to preserve its pristine beauty. It is advisable to dress warmly, as the weather in Iceland can be unpredictable even during summer months.

Overall, Jökulsárlón Glacier Lagoon offers a remarkable blend of natural beauty, glacial wonders, and a serene atmosphere. It stands as a testament to the breathtaking landscapes that Iceland is known for, attracting visitors from around the world who seek to witness the magic of this extraordinary place.

Vatnajokull National Park

Vatnajökull National Park is a stunning natural wonder located in southeastern Iceland. Established in 2008, it is the largest national park in Europe, covering an area of over 14,000 square kilometres (5,400 square miles). The park is named after Vatnajökull, which is the largest glacier in Europe and covers a significant portion of the park's territory.

Vatnajökull National Park is renowned for its breathtaking landscapes, characterised by a diverse range of natural features. The park encompasses glaciers, volcanoes, geothermal areas, ice caves, waterfalls, and vast stretches of unspoiled wilderness. It is a paradise for nature lovers, adventurers, and outdoor enthusiasts.

One of the most iconic features of Vatnajökull National Park is the Vatnajökull glacier itself. Spanning an area of approximately 8,100 square kilometers (3,100 square miles), it is an awe-inspiring sight to behold. The glacier's ice cap is several hundred meters thick in some places, and it conceals numerous volcanic peaks and subglacial volcanoes beneath its icy surface.

Exploring the glacier is a popular activity in the park. Visitors can participate in glacier hiking or ice climbing tours, where they can witness the incredible ice formations, deep crevasses, and vibrant blue ice caves. These ice caves, formed during the winter months, offer a surreal and enchanting experience as light filters through the translucent ice, creating a magical ambiance.

Vatnajökull National Park is also home to several volcanoes, including Öræfajökull, which is the tallest volcano in Iceland. The volcanic landscape is dotted with imposing mountains, rugged lava fields, and steaming geothermal areas. The region's geothermal activity gives rise to hot springs, geysers, and bubbling mud pools, adding to the park's unique charm.

The park is abundant in diverse wildlife, both on land and in its surrounding waters. Various bird species, such as puffins, geese, and swans, can be spotted in the park, especially during the summer months when they come to breed. Marine life, including seals and whales, can also be seen along the nearby coastline.

Vatnajökull National Park offers a range of recreational activities for visitors. Hiking trails wind through the park's picturesque landscapes, allowing explorers to witness the raw beauty of the area. Camping, birdwatching, photography, and fishing are other popular activities enjoyed within the park. During the winter, the park becomes a playground for winter sports enthusiasts, with opportunities for skiing, snowboarding, and snowmobiling.

To preserve the fragile ecosystem, certain areas of the park may have restricted access or require guided tours. It is essential to respect the park's regulations and guidelines to ensure the conservation of its natural wonders.

Vatnajökull National Park truly showcases the magnificent power of nature and provides a once-in-a-lifetime experience for visitors. Whether you're seeking adventure, tranquillity, or a deep connection with the natural world, this Icelandic gem promises to captivate your senses and leave you with memories that will last a lifetime.

CHAPTER 6. Discovering the Stunning Westfjords

Introduction to the Westfjords

The Westfjords in Iceland is a stunning and remote region located in the northwestern part of the country. Known for its dramatic landscapes, rugged coastlines, and rich cultural heritage, the Westfjords offer a unique and untouched experience for visitors.

The Westfjords are characterised by their fjords, deep valleys carved by ancient glaciers, which provide a spectacular backdrop for exploration. The region is sparsely populated, with small fishing villages and towns dotting the coastline. The isolation of the Westfjords contributes to its charm, offering a sense of tranquillity and a chance to connect with nature.

One of the most iconic attractions in the Westfjords is the Dynjandi waterfall, often referred to as the "Queen of Icelandic Waterfalls." This majestic cascade plunges down a series of terraces, creating a mesmerising sight. Visitors can hike along the trail leading to the waterfall, enjoying breathtaking views of the surrounding mountains and fjords.

Another must-see destination in the Westfjords is Hornstrandir Nature Reserve, a pristine wilderness area that is accessible only by boat or on foot. This remote and unspoiled paradise is home to a variety of wildlife, including Arctic foxes, seals, and numerous bird species. Hiking trails crisscross the reserve, allowing nature enthusiasts to explore its rugged beauty.

For those interested in history and culture, the Westfjords offer several interesting sites. The fishing village of Isafjordur, the largest town in the region, is known for its colourful houses, charming harbour, and a vibrant arts scene. The Maritime Museum in Isafjordur provides insights into the area's maritime heritage and the lives of fishermen.

The Westfjords are also a haven for birdwatchers, as the region is home to countless seabirds, including puffins, guillemots, and kittiwakes. The cliffs and cliff sides along the coastline serve as nesting grounds for these magnificent creatures, providing ample opportunities for birdwatching and photography.

In terms of outdoor activities, the Westfjords offer a wide range of options. From hiking and camping to kayaking and whale watching, adventure seekers will find plenty to keep them engaged. The untouched nature and rugged terrain make the region an ideal destination for outdoor enthusiasts looking for a true wilderness experience.

Although the Westfjords may be more remote compared to other popular tourist destinations in Iceland, the journey to this hidden gem is well worth it. Its raw beauty, rich wildlife, and untouched landscapes make it a captivating region for those seeking an off-the-beaten-path adventure. Whether you are an avid hiker, a nature lover, or a cultural enthusiast, the Westfjords will leave you with unforgettable memories and a deep appreciation for Iceland's natural wonders.

Dynjandi Waterfall

Dynjandi Waterfall, also known as Fjallfoss or Thunderous Fall, is a magnificent natural wonder located in the Westfjords region of Iceland. Considered one of the most impressive waterfalls in the country, Dynjandi is a captivating sight that captivates visitors with its awe-inspiring beauty and powerful cascades.

Situated in the remote and untouched landscapes of the Dynjandi Bay, the waterfall is nestled within the Dynjandisá River, which originates from the vast Dynjandisheiði plateau. The river descends over a series of steps, creating a tiered formation that spans approximately 100 metres in height and 60 metres in width.

What sets Dynjandi apart from other waterfalls in Iceland is its sheer scale and elegance. The main cascade at the top is the largest one, plunging down in a single free fall that tapers as it descends. The water then splits into multiple smaller streams as it flows down the subsequent levels, creating a beautiful fan-like shape that resembles a bridal veil.

The sheer power and thunderous roar of the waterfall are awe-inspiring, hence its name "Thunderous Fall." The mist created by the cascading water gives the surroundings a mystical atmosphere, adding to the overall enchantment of the place. The combination of the imposing cliffs, lush green vegetation, and the crystal-clear waters makes Dynjandi an absolute feast for the eyes.

The area around Dynjandi is rich in flora and fauna, and visitors can enjoy exploring the vibrant wildflowers and moss-covered rocks as they make their way up the hiking trail that leads to the top of the waterfall. The hike offers breathtaking views of the surrounding fjords and mountains, providing an opportunity to immerse oneself in Iceland's raw and untouched natural beauty.

Dynjandi Waterfall is not only a visual delight but also a cultural and historical treasure. It has been a prominent landmark in Icelandic folklore and has inspired numerous stories and legends. The waterfall has also been an important source of sustenance for the local communities throughout history, providing a reliable supply of fresh water and fish.

For those who appreciate the beauty of nature, visiting Dynjandi Waterfall is an unforgettable experience. It showcases the raw power and grandeur of Iceland's natural wonders, leaving visitors in awe of the Earth's incredible ability to sculpt breathtaking landscapes.

Hornstrandir Nature Reserve

Hornstrandir Nature Reserve is a stunning and remote wilderness area located in the northwestern region of Iceland. It is renowned for its breathtaking landscapes, rugged cliffs, and diverse wildlife, making it a popular destination for nature lovers and outdoor enthusiasts.

Hornstrandir is situated on the edge of the Arctic Circle and covers approximately 580 square kilometres (225 square miles) of unspoiled beauty. What sets it apart from other nature reserves in Iceland is its untouched and untamed character, as it remains largely uninhabited by humans. The area was officially designated as a nature reserve in 1975 to protect its unique ecosystems and fragile biodiversity.

One of the remarkable features of Hornstrandir is its dramatic and rugged coastline. Towering cliffs, sheer sea stacks, and deep fjords create a mesmerising panorama. Visitors can explore the area's stunning sea caves, arches, and towering bird cliffs, which are home to various seabird species, including puffins, razorbills, guillemots, and kittiwakes. These birds thrive in the remote and undisturbed environment, creating a spectacular display of nature's wonders.

Hornstrandir's inland areas are equally captivating. Vast stretches of untouched wilderness are dominated by lush valleys, meandering rivers, and imposing mountains. Hikers and adventurers can embark on multi-day treks and explore the network of trails that crisscross the reserve. The terrain varies from gentle slopes to challenging mountain peaks, offering a range of options for outdoor enthusiasts of different skill levels.

Wildlife enthusiasts will find Hornstrandir to be a haven for unique and rare species. Arctic foxes, which are the only land mammals native to Iceland, thrive in the reserve's pristine environment. Visitors may have the opportunity to observe these charming creatures in their natural habitat. Additionally, seals, whales, and a variety of seabirds are commonly spotted along the coastline and in the surrounding waters.

Due to its remote location and rugged terrain, Hornstrandir is not easily accessible. There are no roads or permanent settlements within the reserve, making it a true wilderness experience. The most common way to reach Hornstrandir is by taking a boat from Ísafjörður, the largest town in the Westfjords region of Iceland. Guided tours and organised hikes are available for those who want to explore the reserve under the guidance of experienced local operators.

Visiting Hornstrandir Nature Reserve offers a unique opportunity to immerse oneself in Iceland's raw and untamed beauty. Its pristine landscapes, abundant wildlife, and sense of solitude make it a remarkable destination for nature enthusiasts seeking a genuine wilderness experience.

Látrabjarg Cliff

Látrabjarg Cliff is an impressive natural wonder located on the westernmost point of Iceland's Westfjords region. Stretching for about 14 kilometres along the coastline, Látrabjarg is renowned for its dramatic cliffs, stunning views, and its significance as a nesting site for numerous seabird species.

The cliffs of Látrabjarg rise vertically from the North Atlantic Ocean, reaching heights of up to 440 metres (1,440 feet) in some places. These towering cliffs create a mesmerising spectacle, particularly when viewed from the ocean or from the top, offering panoramic vistas of the surrounding coastal landscapes.

Látrabjarg is internationally recognized as a prime location for birdwatching. It is home to one of the largest seabird colonies in the world, attracting millions of birds during the breeding season. Some of the notable bird species that nest here include puffins, guillemots, razorbills, fulmars, and kittiwakes. Bird enthusiasts and photographers flock to Látrabjarg to witness these fascinating creatures up close and capture memorable images.

One of the most iconic and beloved inhabitants of Látrabjarg is the Atlantic puffin. These charismatic seabirds arrive in late April and May to breed, digging burrows in the cliffside where they lay their eggs. Puffins are known for their vibrant beaks, striking black and white plumage, and their comical, clumsy flight patterns. Watching them interact and observing their nesting behaviours is a highlight for many visitors.

Aside from birdwatching, Látrabjarg Cliff offers other attractions and activities. The scenic surroundings provide excellent opportunities for hiking and walking along the cliff edge, immersing visitors in the raw beauty of the Icelandic landscape. However, it is essential to exercise caution near the cliff edges due to their steep drop-offs.

Látrabjarg's remote location contributes to its unique charm. The area is relatively isolated and less visited compared to other popular tourist destinations in Iceland. This remoteness enhances the sense of tranquillity and untouched nature, allowing visitors to experience a peaceful retreat away from the crowds.

To reach Látrabjarg, one must venture along the winding roads of the Westfjords, which can be challenging due to the region's rugged terrain. However, the journey is undoubtedly rewarding for those seeking an off-the-beaten-path adventure.

In summary, Látrabjarg Cliff in Iceland is a majestic natural landmark celebrated for its awe-inspiring cliffs, breathtaking views, and abundant birdlife. It offers a captivating experience for nature enthusiasts, photographers, and anyone seeking an extraordinary encounter with Iceland's remarkable landscapes and wildlife.

Remote Villages and Local Culture

Iceland, known as the "Land of Fire and Ice," is a country renowned for its stunning landscapes, geothermal wonders, and unique cultural heritage. While Iceland has a small population, it is also home to several remote villages that offer a glimpse into the country's local culture and traditions.

One of the remarkable aspects of remote villages in Iceland is their isolation and connection to nature. Many of these villages are nestled in breathtaking natural settings, surrounded by mountains, fjords, and vast expanses of untouched wilderness. The remote locations often mean limited access to amenities and services, creating a strong sense of self-reliance and resilience among the local communities.

In these villages, traditional Icelandic culture thrives. The inhabitants have a deep appreciation for their heritage and actively preserve their cultural practices. Language, folklore, and storytelling play significant roles in maintaining and passing down traditions from one generation to the next.

Traditional Icelandic cuisine is also prevalent in these remote areas. Locally sourced ingredients, such as fish, lamb, and dairy products, form the basis of many dishes. You may find delightful specialties like fermented shark (hákarl), smoked lamb (hangikjöt), and the famous Icelandic hot spring bread (hverabrauð), which is baked underground using geothermal heat.

Music is an integral part of Icelandic culture, and remote villages often have their own local musicians and bands. Traditional Icelandic folk music, with its haunting melodies and poetic lyrics, is cherished, but contemporary music genres are also embraced. The annual Þjóðhátturinn, a national singing competition, showcases the diversity and talent of Icelandic music across the country, including in remote areas.

Another significant aspect of local culture in Iceland is the presence of sagas. These ancient Icelandic sagas are historical and literary narratives that tell stories of the country's early settlers and heroes. Many remote villages have connections to these sagas, and their inhabitants take pride in their historical ties and the legacies left by their ancestors.

One remote village worth mentioning is Seyðisfjörður, located in the eastern part of Iceland. This picturesque village is nestled within a fjord and is renowned for its vibrant arts scene. The town hosts an annual arts festival, attracting artists from Iceland and abroad to showcase their work. The local community actively participates in various cultural events, fostering a creative and lively atmosphere.

In addition to cultural experiences, remote villages in Iceland offer opportunities for outdoor activities and exploration. The natural surroundings provide a haven for hikers, birdwatchers, and nature enthusiasts. Remote villages often serve as gateways to breathtaking landscapes, including glaciers, volcanoes, and waterfalls.

Visiting these remote villages allows you to experience Iceland's local culture firsthand and witness the unique way of life that has developed in harmony with the country's awe-inspiring natural wonders. Whether it's connecting with the friendly locals, immersing yourself in traditional music and cuisine, or exploring the untamed landscapes, remote villages in Iceland offer a truly enriching and authentic experience.

CHAPTER 7. The Magical Northern Lights

Understanding the Northern Lights

The Northern Lights, also known as the Aurora Borealis, are a mesmerising natural phenomenon that occurs in high-latitude regions, including Iceland. Iceland is renowned for its stunning displays of the Northern Lights, attracting visitors from around the world who seek to witness this ethereal spectacle.

Understanding the Northern Lights begins with grasping the scientific explanation behind this magical display. The Northern Lights are caused by charged particles from the sun colliding with atoms and molecules in the Earth's atmosphere. These charged particles, predominantly electrons and protons, are carried by the solar wind, a stream of charged particles constantly emanating from the sun.

When the solar wind reaches the Earth's magnetic field, it interacts with the magnetosphere, creating a highly charged region near the poles. As the charged particles spiral along the Earth's magnetic field lines, they collide with atmospheric particles, such as oxygen and nitrogen. These collisions excite the atoms and molecules, causing them to release energy in the form of colourful light.

The vibrant hues of the Northern Lights are a result of the different atmospheric elements involved. Oxygen produces green and red lights, while nitrogen contributes to blue and purple shades. The specific colors visible in the sky depend on the altitude at which the collisions occur and the types of atoms or molecules involved.

Iceland's geographical location makes it an excellent vantage point for witnessing the Northern Lights. The country's position near the Arctic Circle places it within the auroral oval, an area encircling the Earth's magnetic poles where the Northern Lights are most frequently observed. The combination of dark winter nights and minimal light pollution in many rural areas of Iceland enhances the viewing experience, providing optimal conditions to appreciate the brilliance of the auroras.

To increase your chances of witnessing the Northern Lights in Iceland, it is recommended to visit between September and April, when the nights are longer and darker. It's essential to check weather conditions and solar activity forecasts, as clear skies and heightened solar activity significantly enhance the visibility of the auroras. Many tour operators in Iceland offer Northern Lights tours, taking visitors to prime locations away from light pollution and providing expert guides who can explain the phenomenon in greater detail.

It's important to note that the Northern Lights are a natural phenomenon and can be unpredictable. Even with the best planning and favourable conditions, there is no guarantee of seeing them on any given night. However, the awe-inspiring landscapes of Iceland, combined with the potential for experiencing the Northern Lights, make it an enchanting destination for those seeking to understand and appreciate the beauty of this celestial spectacle.

Best Time and Locations for Viewing

Iceland is known for its breathtaking natural landscapes, including stunning displays of the Northern Lights, also known as the Aurora Borealis. To have the best chance of witnessing this mesmerising phenomenon, it's important to consider the best time and locations for viewing in Iceland.

1. Time of Year:
The best time to see the Northern Lights in Iceland is during the winter months, from September to April. This period offers long nights and clear, dark skies, which are ideal conditions for observing the auroras. However, keep in mind that the peak months for Northern Lights activity are usually from October to March.

2. Weather Conditions:
Clear skies are essential for optimal Northern Lights viewing. Choose a night when the weather forecast predicts minimal cloud cover. Keep an eye on the aurora forecasts and local weather updates to increase your chances of a successful viewing experience.

3. Darkness:
The darker the location, the better your chances of seeing the Northern Lights. Try to find areas away from city lights and light pollution. Rural locations, national parks, and remote areas are excellent choices. The more isolated you are from artificial

light sources, the more vibrant and visible the auroras will be.

4. Ideal Locations:
a. Reykjavik: Despite being the capital city, Reykjavik can still offer decent Northern Lights displays, especially during strong solar activity. Areas such as Öskjuhlíð Hill and Grótta Lighthouse, located on the outskirts of the city, provide darker skies.

b. South Coast: The south coast of Iceland offers diverse landscapes and great potential for Northern Lights viewing. Areas like Vík, Skógafoss, and Jökulsárlón Glacier Lagoon provide stunning backdrops for aurora sightings.

c. Snæfellsnes Peninsula: Known as "Iceland in miniature," Snæfellsnes Peninsula offers picturesque landscapes and dark skies. Kirkjufell Mountain and the surrounding areas are popular spots for Northern Lights photography.

d. Westfjords: The remote and sparsely populated Westfjords region provides excellent opportunities for viewing the Northern Lights. Towns like Ísafjörður and Patreksfjörður are good starting points.

e. Lake Mývatn: Located in northern Iceland, Lake Mývatn is renowned for its geothermal activity and stunning surroundings. The lake area offers dark skies and fewer crowds, making it an excellent location for aurora hunting.

Remember that the Northern Lights are a natural phenomenon, and their appearance cannot be guaranteed. Patience and persistence are key, as the lights can be elusive and may require multiple attempts to witness. It's advisable to join organized Northern Lights tours or consult with local guides who can provide up-to-date information and increase your chances of experiencing this awe-inspiring spectacle.

Photography Tips and Techniques

Iceland is a stunning destination for photographers, with its dramatic landscapes, glaciers, waterfalls, and unique light conditions. Whether you're a professional or an amateur photographer, capturing the beauty of Iceland requires some planning and knowledge. Here are some photography tips and techniques to help you make the most of your photography experience in Iceland:

1. Golden Hours: Take advantage of the unique lighting conditions in Iceland, especially during the golden hours, which occur around sunrise and sunset. The low angle of the sun during these times creates soft, warm light and long shadows, enhancing the textures and colours of the landscape.

2. Weather and Seasons: Be prepared for changing weather conditions in Iceland, as it can be unpredictable. Pack layers of clothing, waterproof gear, and sturdy shoes to protect yourself and your equipment. Each season in Iceland offers its own unique photographic opportunities, so research the best time to visit based on the kind of images you want to capture.

3. Composition: Iceland's landscapes are vast and diverse, offering endless composition possibilities. Pay attention to foreground elements such as rocks, vegetation, or ice formations to create depth and add interest to your photos. Experiment with different angles, leading lines, and the rule of thirds to create visually appealing compositions.

4. Waterfalls: Iceland is renowned for its breathtaking waterfalls. When photographing waterfalls, use a tripod to capture long exposure

shots, which can create a silky, ethereal effect as the water flows. Experiment with different shutter speeds to achieve the desired level of smoothness or motion in the water.

5. Glacier Photography: Iceland is home to numerous glaciers, presenting unique photographic opportunities. When photographing glaciers, consider including a human element or an object for scale, as it helps convey the immense size and beauty of the glaciers. Be cautious when venturing onto glaciers and always prioritise safety.

6. Night Photography: Iceland's dark skies and minimal light pollution make it an excellent destination for night photography. If you're interested in capturing the Northern Lights (Aurora Borealis), visit Iceland during the winter months. Use a sturdy tripod, a wide-angle lens, and a high ISO setting to capture the mesmerising dance of the lights.

7. Wildlife: Iceland is home to diverse wildlife, including puffins, seals, reindeer, and whales. Research the best locations and seasons for wildlife photography and respect the animals' natural habitat. Use a telephoto lens for wildlife

photography to capture detailed and intimate shots while maintaining a safe distance.

8. Post-processing: Once you've captured your images, post-processing can help enhance the final results. Experiment with editing software to fine-tune exposure, colour balance, and sharpness while maintaining a natural look. Remember to retain the essence of the scene and avoid excessive editing that can lead to unrealistic results.

Remember, while photography is about capturing beautiful images, it's equally important to enjoy the experience and immerse yourself in the awe-inspiring landscapes that Iceland has to offer. Respect the environment, follow any local regulations, and always prioritise safety while exploring and photographing this remarkable country.

CHAPTER 8. Outdoor Adventures and Activities

Hiking and Trekking

Iceland is a haven for outdoor enthusiasts, offering breathtaking landscapes and a multitude of hiking and trekking opportunities. With its rugged terrain, stunning glaciers, volcanoes, and cascading waterfalls, Iceland provides a unique and unforgettable experience for hikers and trekkers of all levels.

One of the most famous long-distance hiking trails in Iceland is the Laugavegur Trail. Stretching approximately 55 kilometres (34 miles) through the Icelandic Highlands, this trail takes you through a diverse range of landscapes, including colorful mountains, geothermal hot springs, glacial valleys, and black sand deserts. The trail typically takes four to six days to complete and offers stunning views of Iceland's natural wonders.

Another popular hiking destination is the Snæfellsnes Peninsula, located in western Iceland. Often referred to as "Iceland in miniature," Snæfellsnes offers a condensed version of the country's diverse landscapes, including majestic mountains, lava fields, sea cliffs, and the iconic Snæfellsjökull glacier-capped volcano. Hiking trails on the peninsula cater to various skill levels, providing opportunities for both short day hikes and longer multi-day treks.

For those seeking a more challenging adventure, Iceland's interior highlands provide an array of options. The Fimmvörðuháls Trek is a demanding but rewarding trail that takes you from the famous Skógafoss waterfall to the stunning Þórsmörk valley. This 25-kilometre (15.5-mile) trail traverses glaciers, lava fields, and volcanic landscapes, offering panoramic views of the surrounding area.

If you're interested in exploring Iceland's glaciers, the Skaftafell National Park is a must-visit destination. Located in the southern part of the country, this park features numerous hiking trails that lead to awe-inspiring glaciers, such as the mighty Vatnajökull, Europe's largest ice cap. Guided glacier hikes are available for those who want to venture onto the ice and experience the frozen world up close.

When planning a hiking or trekking trip in Iceland, it's important to consider the weather and safety precautions. Iceland's weather can be unpredictable, and conditions can change rapidly, so it's crucial to be well-prepared with appropriate gear, clothing, and provisions. Additionally, it's recommended to inform someone about your hiking plans and check weather and trail conditions before setting out.

Iceland's untouched natural beauty and unique landscapes make it a remarkable destination for hiking and trekking. Whether you choose to explore the iconic trails, venture into the highlands, or hike along the glacier-filled valleys, Iceland offers a wealth of opportunities to immerse yourself in its awe-inspiring scenery and create unforgettable memories.

Glacier Tours and Ice Climbing

Glacier tours and ice climbing in Iceland offer exhilarating and unforgettable experiences in one of the world's most stunning natural environments. Iceland is known for its breathtaking landscapes, and its glaciers are among the most captivating features of the country.

Glacier tours provide an opportunity to explore and appreciate the icy wonders of Iceland up close.

These tours typically take place on one of the country's largest glaciers, such as Vatnajökull, Langjökull, or Snæfellsjökull. Knowledgeable guides lead the tours, ensuring safety and providing interesting information about the glaciers, their formation, and their significance to the local environment.

During a glacier tour, visitors can witness the awe-inspiring beauty of ice formations, including ice caves, crevasses, and icefalls. The glacier's constantly changing nature means that no two tours are the same, making each excursion a unique adventure. The stunning blue ice, created by the compression of snow over centuries, adds a magical touch to the experience.

Ice climbing is a thrilling activity that allows participants to challenge themselves physically and mentally while scaling the vertical ice walls of a glacier. Whether you are a seasoned climber or a beginner, there are options available to suit different skill levels. Professional guides provide instruction and safety equipment, ensuring a safe and enjoyable climbing experience.

Glacier tours and ice climbing in Iceland are suitable for individuals, families, or groups who are seeking an unforgettable adventure amidst nature's icy wonders. These activities offer a chance to connect with Iceland's raw and unspoiled landscapes, showcasing the country's unique geology and natural beauty.

It's important to note that glacier tours and ice climbing involve some inherent risks due to the unpredictable nature of glaciers. Therefore, it is essential to follow the guidance of experienced guides, adhere to safety protocols, and use appropriate equipment to ensure a safe and enjoyable experience.

Iceland's glaciers are a precious resource that is vulnerable to the effects of climate change. It is crucial to approach these activities with a mindset of environmental responsibility and respect for nature. Tour operators and guides in Iceland often emphasise sustainable practices, such as leaving no trace and minimising their ecological footprint, to protect the fragile glacial environment.

Overall, glacier tours and ice climbing in Iceland offer a unique opportunity to explore the icy wonders of this remarkable country. Whether you choose to witness the stunning landscapes on a guided tour or challenge yourself with ice climbing, these activities provide unforgettable experiences and a deeper appreciation for the raw beauty of Iceland's glaciers.

Whale Watching

Whale watching in Iceland is an incredible experience that attracts thousands of visitors each year. Iceland is renowned as one of the best places in the world to observe whales due to its unique geographical location and rich marine ecosystems. The country's cold waters and nutrient-rich currents create a perfect habitat for various species of whales, making it a prime destination for whale enthusiasts.

Several locations around Iceland offer whale watching tours, including Reykjavik, Husavik, Akureyri, and Dalvík. These tours typically take visitors out into the open ocean, where they have the opportunity to see these majestic creatures up close in their natural environment.

Iceland is home to several species of whales, including the humpback whale, minke whale, blue whale, fin whale, and orca (also known as killer whale). The humpback whale is particularly popular among tourists due to its acrobatic displays, such as breaching and tail slapping. These gentle giants can grow up to 50 feet in length and are known for their distinct songs, which are often heard during whale watching excursions.

Husavik, located in northern Iceland, is often referred to as the "whale watching capital" of the country. It offers a higher chance of spotting whales due to its proximity to prime feeding grounds. The town is also home to the Husavik Whale Museum, which provides educational insights into the biology and behaviour of these magnificent creatures.

When planning a whale watching trip in Iceland, it's essential to choose a reputable tour operator that follows responsible whale watching practices. These operators prioritise the well-being of the whales and adhere to guidelines to minimise disturbance to their natural habitat. They also provide knowledgeable guides who share information about the whales and the surrounding marine environment.

It's important to note that whale sightings are never guaranteed, as these are wild animals in their natural habitat. However, the chances of spotting whales in Iceland are generally high, and even if you don't encounter them, the breathtaking landscapes and seascapes of the country make the trip worthwhile.

In addition to whale watching, Iceland offers various other attractions and activities for visitors to enjoy. You can explore stunning waterfalls, geothermal hot springs, volcanic landscapes, and picturesque coastal towns. The unique combination of natural beauty and the opportunity to witness these magnificent marine mammals makes whale watching in Iceland an unforgettable experience.

Hot Springs and Geothermal Baths

Iceland is renowned for its geothermal activity, which provides a unique opportunity to experience hot springs and geothermal baths throughout the country. The island's geology, characterised by volcanoes, geysers, and hot springs, offers locals and visitors a chance to unwind and relax in naturally heated waters, surrounded by breathtaking landscapes.

Hot springs are abundant in Iceland and are often found in geothermal areas, where underground volcanic activity brings hot water to the surface. These geothermal areas are spread across the country, with some of the most famous ones located in the southwestern region, the Golden Circle route, and the northern part of Iceland.

The Blue Lagoon is perhaps the most iconic geothermal spa in Iceland. Situated in a lava field on the Reykjanes Peninsula, close to the Keflavik International Airport, it offers visitors a unique bathing experience. The milky blue, mineral-rich waters are rich in silica and sulphur, providing various health benefits. The Blue Lagoon also features saunas, steam baths, and in-water massage services, making it a popular destination for relaxation and rejuvenation.

Another popular hot spring in Iceland is the Mývatn Nature Baths, located in the northern part of the country. These geothermal baths offer a more serene and less crowded experience compared to the Blue Lagoon. Surrounded by volcanic landscapes and with water temperatures reaching around 36-40°C (97-104°F), the Mývatn Nature Baths provide a tranquil retreat for visitors.

In addition to these well-known hot springs, Iceland is dotted with numerous smaller geothermal baths and hot pots. These can be found both in popular tourist areas and off the beaten path, offering a more intimate and local experience.

Many of these baths are free to access, allowing visitors to immerse themselves in nature while enjoying the warm waters.

It's important to note that when visiting hot springs and geothermal baths, it's essential to follow the guidelines and rules provided at each location. These guidelines ensure the preservation of the natural environment and the safety of visitors. It's also important to shower without a swimsuit before entering the hot springs, as it helps maintain the water's cleanliness.

Overall, hot springs and geothermal baths in Iceland provide a unique opportunity to relax and unwind while immersing yourself in the country's stunning natural landscapes. Whether you choose to visit well-known sites like the Blue Lagoon or explore lesser-known local hot pots, the experience is sure to be both invigorating and soothing.

Horseback Riding and Bird Watching

Horseback riding and bird watching in Iceland offer unique and thrilling experiences for nature enthusiasts. Iceland's diverse landscapes, including its volcanic terrain, glaciers, waterfalls, and vast open spaces, make it an ideal destination for exploring on horseback and observing a variety of bird species.

Horseback riding is deeply ingrained in Icelandic culture and has been a tradition for centuries. The Icelandic horse, a breed known for its strength, endurance, and gentle temperament, is the perfect companion for exploring the country's rugged terrain. Riders can embark on guided tours that cater to all skill levels, from beginners to experienced equestrians.

Iceland's dramatic landscapes provide a stunning backdrop for horseback riding adventures. Riding through moss-covered lava fields, crossing glacial rivers, or traversing black sand beaches creates an unforgettable experience. The Icelandic horse's unique gait, known as the tölt, offers a smooth and comfortable ride, allowing riders to enjoy the breathtaking scenery while feeling connected to nature.

Bird watching is another popular activity in Iceland, thanks to the country's rich birdlife and diverse habitats. Iceland serves as a vital breeding ground and migratory stopover for numerous bird species.

The country's unspoiled wilderness provides sanctuary for various seabirds, waterfowl, and waders.

One of the most renowned bird watching sites in Iceland is Lake Mývatn, located in the north of the country. It is a designated nature reserve and home to numerous bird species, including ducks, swans, geese, and rare waders such as the red-necked phalarope. Other coastal areas, such as the Westfjords and the Snæfellsnes Peninsula, are also fantastic bird watching destinations.

Puffins, with their colourful beaks and charming appearance, are among the most beloved birds in Iceland. The Westman Islands, particularly Heimaey, host the largest puffin colonies, providing a unique opportunity to observe these charismatic seabirds up close.

During the summer months, bird watchers can witness the incredible sight of nesting colonies, courtship displays, and fledglings taking their first flights. The midnight sun in Iceland allows for extended bird watching hours, adding to the enchantment of the experience.

To enhance the bird watching experience, local guides and tour operators provide expert knowledge and assistance. They can help identify different bird species, offer insights into their behaviour, and take visitors to prime viewing locations.

It's important to note that both horseback riding and bird watching in Iceland should be conducted with respect for the environment and the wildlife. Visitors should adhere to guidelines and regulations, maintain a safe distance from birds and nesting areas, and prioritise the well-being of Icelandic nature.

Whether you choose to explore Iceland's diverse landscapes on horseback or immerse yourself in the fascinating world of bird watching, these activities offer unforgettable adventures in a country renowned for its natural beauty.

CHAPTER 9. Wildlife and Nature Reserves

Snaefellsnes Peninsula

The Snæfellsnes Peninsula is a stunning region located on the western coast of Iceland. Known for its dramatic landscapes, diverse natural features, and mystical ambiance, it has become a popular destination for tourists seeking to explore Iceland's untamed beauty.

One of the most prominent features of the Snæfellsnes Peninsula is the Snæfellsjökull volcano, an active stratovolcano that towers over the peninsula. It gained fame as the setting for Jules Verne's novel "Journey to the Center of the Earth," where it served as the entrance to a subterranean world. Snæfellsjökull is covered by a glacier, and its imposing presence adds to the peninsula's allure.

The Snæfellsnes Peninsula offers a wide range of natural wonders. Its coastline is dotted with picturesque fishing villages, such as Arnarstapi and Hellnar, where visitors can immerse themselves in the traditional Icelandic way of life and enjoy fresh seafood delicacies. These villages also provide access to stunning coastal cliffs, black sand beaches, and sea caves carved by the relentless waves of the North Atlantic Ocean.

Venturing further inland, visitors will discover a landscape of rugged mountains, volcanic craters, and lava fields. The Kirkjufell mountain and its iconic cone-shaped peak have become one of Iceland's most photographed landmarks. The mountain is often called "The Church Mountain" due to its resemblance to a church steeple.

The Snæfellsnes Peninsula is also rich in wildlife. Birdwatchers will be delighted by the abundance of seabirds, including puffins, guillemots, and kittiwakes, which nest along the cliffs and sea stacks. The waters surrounding the peninsula are home to seals and occasionally visited by whales, making it a fantastic spot for marine wildlife enthusiasts.

Hiking and outdoor activities are popular on the Snæfellsnes Peninsula, offering visitors the chance to explore its captivating landscapes up close. The area boasts several well-marked trails, ranging from leisurely coastal walks to challenging mountain hikes. The varied terrain provides ample opportunities for photography, with each turn revealing a new breathtaking vista.

Additionally, the Snæfellsnes Peninsula is steeped in folklore and legends, with many Icelanders believing it to be an area of powerful energy and spiritual significance. The mystical aura surrounding Snæfellsjökull volcano has inspired artists, writers, and mystics for centuries, making it a magnet for those seeking a connection with nature and the supernatural.

Whether you're an adventure seeker, nature lover, or history enthusiast, the Snæfellsnes Peninsula in Iceland offers a mesmerising blend of beauty, tranquillity, and mystery. Its captivating landscapes, rich wildlife, and mythical allure make it an unforgettable destination for travellers seeking an authentic Icelandic experience.

Lake Myvatn and the Dimmuborgir Lava Fields

Lake Mývatn and the Dimmuborgir Lava Fields are two iconic natural attractions located in northeastern Iceland. They are known for their stunning landscapes, unique geological formations, and rich biodiversity. Let's explore each of them in more detail:

1. Lake Mývatn:
Lake Mývatn is a picturesque lake situated in the Mývatn region of northern Iceland. It is renowned for its diverse birdlife and geothermal activity. The name "Mývatn" translates to "Midge Lake" due to the swarms of midges that inhabit the area during the summer months, attracting numerous bird species. Birdwatching enthusiasts flock to this area to observe the wide array of bird species, including ducks, geese, and waders.

The surrounding landscape of Lake Mývatn is a striking mix of volcanic craters, geothermal vents, and pseudocraters. These pseudocraters, known as Skútustaðagígar, were formed when hot lava flowed over wetlands, causing steam explosions that created the distinctive circular formations seen today. Exploring these craters provides visitors with a unique insight into the geological processes that have shaped the area.

Another noteworthy feature near Lake Mývatn is the geothermal area of Námaskarð. It is characterised by steaming fumaroles, bubbling mud pots, and vibrant mineral deposits, creating an otherworldly and surreal atmosphere. The contrasting colours and the powerful release of steam make it a fascinating place to visit.

2. Dimmuborgir Lava Fields:
Located east of Lake Mývatn, the Dimmuborgir Lava Fields are a magnificent labyrinth of lava formations, caves, and rock pillars. The name "Dimmuborgir" translates to "Dark Cities" or "Dark Castles," aptly describing the eerie and mystical atmosphere of this place.

These lava formations were created during a volcanic eruption around 2,300 years ago when molten lava flowed over the area, forming intricate patterns and sculptures. As the lava cooled and solidified, it created a network of towering pillars and arches, reminiscent of a chaotic and haunting cityscape.

Exploring the Dimmuborgir Lava Fields allows visitors to wander through narrow passages and admire the unique shapes and formations created by the lava. The most famous structure is the "Kirkjan" or "The Church," a large cavern with towering walls that resembles a gothic cathedral.

The Dimmuborgir Lava Fields also hold a prominent place in Icelandic folklore. According to legends, it is believed to be the dwelling place of trolls and other mythical creatures, further adding to its enchanting appeal.

Both Lake Mývatn and the Dimmuborgir Lava Fields offer visitors a chance to witness the raw beauty of Iceland's geology and natural wonders. Whether you're captivated by the diverse birdlife around the lake or fascinated by the mysterious lava formations, these attractions provide a memorable experience that showcases Iceland's extraordinary landscapes.

Puffin Colonies

Iceland is renowned for its stunning landscapes, including its vibrant wildlife. One of the fascinating sights in Iceland is the presence of puffin colonies along its coastlines. Puffins, also known as "clowns of the sea," are seabirds that nest in large numbers on coastal cliffs and islands.

Iceland provides ideal breeding grounds for puffins due to its abundant food supply in the surrounding waters. These charming birds spend most of their lives at sea, but during the breeding season, they return to land to form colonies and raise their young.

Puffin colonies in Iceland are found in various locations around the country, particularly along the southern and western coasts. Some notable places where puffins gather in significant numbers include the Westman Islands (Vestmannaeyjar), Dyrhólaey, Látrabjarg, and the Hornstrandir Nature Reserve.

The Westman Islands, located off the south coast of Iceland, are home to one of the largest puffin colonies in the country. Here, visitors can witness thousands of puffins nesting on steep cliffs, creating a remarkable spectacle. The islands' volcanic landscape and picturesque cliffs add to the allure of observing these delightful birds.

Dyrhólaey, a prominent cape along Iceland's southern coast, is another popular spot to observe puffins. The cliffs of Dyrhólaey provide nesting sites for puffins, and visitors can often see them perched on the ledges or flying in and out of their burrows. The panoramic views from Dyrhólaey, encompassing the black sand beaches and the surrounding ocean, make it an excellent location for birdwatching.

Látrabjarg, located in the Westfjords region, is the westernmost point of Iceland and hosts one of the largest bird cliffs in Europe. Puffins flock to Látrabjarg during the breeding season, creating a bustling colony that stretches for several kilometers. Visitors can observe puffins up close as they go about their daily activities, such as fishing and caring for their chicks.

The Hornstrandir Nature Reserve, located in the remote and rugged Westfjords, offers a more secluded and pristine puffin-watching experience. The cliffs and grassy slopes of the reserve provide ideal nesting habitats for puffins. Exploring this remote area offers a chance to observe puffins in their natural habitat, away from the hustle and bustle of more accessible sites.

When visiting puffin colonies in Iceland, it's important to respect the birds and their environment. Puffins are protected by law in Iceland, and it is forbidden to disturb their nests or harm them in any way. Maintaining a safe distance and avoiding sudden movements ensures the welfare of both the puffins and visitors.

Puffin colonies in Iceland offer a remarkable opportunity to witness these captivating seabirds in their natural habitat. Whether it's their comical appearance, colourful beaks, or their agile flight, puffins never fail to enchant those who have the chance to observe them.

Arctic Foxes and Reindeer

Arctic foxes and reindeer are two fascinating animal species found in Iceland. Despite the harsh and extreme conditions of the Arctic region, these animals have adapted to their environment and play important roles in the country's ecosystem.

Arctic Foxes:
Arctic foxes (Vulpes lagopus) are native to Iceland and can be found throughout the country, including its remote and barren regions. They are well adapted to the Arctic's freezing temperatures, with a thick, warm fur that changes color with the seasons. During the winter, their fur turns white to blend in with the snowy landscape, while in the summer, it changes to a brown or grayish color.

These small carnivores are well-suited to survive in Iceland's challenging environment. They have a compact body shape, which helps minimize heat loss, and their paws are covered in fur, acting as natural snowshoes. Arctic foxes primarily feed on small mammals like voles and birds, as well as scavenging on carcasses left behind by larger predators.

Reindeer:
Reindeer (Rangifer tarandus) were not native to Iceland but were introduced to the country from Norway in the late 18th century. Today, they can be found in various parts of Iceland, mainly in the eastern and northern regions. The Icelandic reindeer population is semi-domesticated, with some herds being privately owned and others considered wild.

These majestic animals are well adapted to the Arctic climate. Their thick coat provides insulation against the cold, and they have large, concave hooves that help them navigate through snow and icy terrain. Reindeer are herbivores, and their diet primarily consists of lichens, grasses, mosses, and shrubs.

Reindeer have cultural significance in Iceland and are often associated with the holiday season. In the wild, they play an important role in the ecosystem by regulating vegetation growth through grazing and dispersing seeds through their droppings.

Conservation:
Both Arctic foxes and reindeer face certain challenges in Iceland. Climate change poses a significant threat to their habitats, as rising temperatures can affect the availability of food and alter the Arctic ecosystem. Human activities, such as hunting and habitat destruction, also impact these species.

Efforts are being made to protect and conserve these animals. Iceland has designated several protected areas to safeguard their habitats, and hunting regulations are in place to ensure sustainable populations. Researchers and conservationists are studying the behaviours and movements of these animals to better understand their needs and develop effective conservation strategies.

Arctic foxes and reindeer are emblematic of Iceland's unique wildlife, showcasing the resilience and adaptability of nature in extreme environments. Their presence adds to the country's natural beauty and serves as a reminder of the delicate balance between humans and the Arctic ecosystem.

CHAPTER 10. Off the Beaten Path

Remote Highlands

The remote highlands of Iceland are an awe-inspiring and rugged region located in the interior part of the country. Known as "Hálendið" in Icelandic, the highlands cover a vast and uninhabited area, offering a unique and untouched wilderness experience for adventurous travellers.

The highlands of Iceland are characterised by their dramatic landscapes, which include volcanoes, geothermal areas, glaciers, vast lava fields, colourful mountains, and expansive deserts. This region is truly a paradise for nature enthusiasts and photographers, as it offers breathtaking vistas and a sense of isolation that is hard to find elsewhere.

One of the remarkable features of the remote highlands is its impressive volcanic activity. The highlands are home to several active and dormant volcanoes, including Askja, Hekla, and Bárðarbunga. These volcanoes have shaped the landscape over centuries, leaving behind vast lava fields and other geological formations that are both fascinating and hauntingly beautiful.

Glaciers also play a significant role in shaping the highland's terrain. Vatnajökull, Europe's largest glacier, dominates the southeastern part of the highlands. Its massive ice cap covers numerous active volcanoes and creates a stunning contrast against the surrounding volcanic landscapes. Other glaciers, such as Langjökull and Hofsjökull, can also be found in the highlands, adding to the region's icy allure.

The highlands are notorious for their challenging and rugged terrain, which necessitates proper preparation and a suitable vehicle for exploration. Most of the area is only accessible by 4x4 vehicles, and some parts are only reachable during the summer months when the snow melts and the rivers become fordable. It is important to note that venturing into the highlands requires careful planning, as the weather can be unpredictable, and the region is devoid of basic facilities such as gas stations or accommodations.

While the highlands are devoid of permanent human settlements, there are a few huts and mountain cabins scattered throughout the region, providing basic shelter for hikers and explorers. These accommodations are usually operated by the Icelandic Touring Association (Ferðafélag Íslands) and require advance bookings.

Exploring the remote highlands offers a sense of solitude and tranquillity rarely found in more populated areas. It is a paradise for hikers, offering numerous trails that take visitors through stunning valleys, along rivers, and up majestic mountains. Landmannalaugar, located in the southern highlands, is a popular starting point for hiking expeditions, and its colourful rhyolite mountains and natural hot springs attract many visitors.

Additionally, the highlands are home to a rich variety of wildlife, including birds, reindeer, and arctic foxes. The region provides important nesting grounds for numerous bird species, making it a haven for birdwatching enthusiasts.

In conclusion, the remote highlands of Iceland offer a mesmerising and untouched natural environment, showcasing the raw power of volcanic activity and the delicate beauty of glaciers. While exploring this remote region requires careful planning and an adventurous spirit, the rewards are unmatched, with breathtaking landscapes, solitude, and a profound connection with nature awaiting those who venture into this unique part of Iceland.

Westman Islands

The Westman Islands, also known as Vestmannaeyjar, is a group of volcanic islands located off the southern coast of Iceland. These islands are situated in the North Atlantic Ocean and are renowned for their stunning natural beauty, unique geology, and rich history.

The largest island in the archipelago is Heimaey, which is also the only inhabited one. Heimaey is home to the town of Vestmannaeyjar, where most of the island's population resides. The town offers a range of amenities and services, including restaurants, accommodations, and shops, making it a popular destination for both locals and tourists.

One of the defining features of the Westman Islands is Eldfell, a volcanic cone that formed during a dramatic eruption in 1973. This eruption led to the evacuation of the entire population, and it had a significant impact on the landscape of Heimaey. Today, visitors can hike up Eldfell to witness the stark contrast between the new lava fields and the surrounding greenery, providing a unique opportunity to witness the power of nature.

In addition to its volcanic landscape, the Westman Islands are also known for their diverse birdlife. The cliffs and sea stacks around the islands are home to numerous seabird colonies, including puffins, guillemots, and kittiwakes. Birdwatching enthusiasts flock to the islands during the summer months to observe these fascinating creatures in their natural habitat.

For those interested in history, the Westman Islands offer a glimpse into Iceland's past. The islands were settled by Irish monks in the 8th century and later became a base for Viking explorers. Over the years, the islands were subject to attacks and raids, and their history is filled with tales of resilience and survival. The Eldheimar Museum on Heimaey provides a fascinating insight into the 1973 volcanic eruption and its impact on the community.

The Westman Islands can be reached by a short ferry ride from the mainland or by a domestic flight from Reykjavik. Once on the islands, visitors can explore the unique landscapes through hiking trails, boat tours, and even by taking part in puffin-watching excursions. The islands also offer opportunities for camping, fishing, and other outdoor activities.

Whether you're interested in natural wonders, birdwatching, history, or outdoor adventures, the Westman Islands in Iceland have something to offer. With their captivating landscapes and intriguing history, these islands provide a truly memorable experience for anyone visiting this beautiful part of the world.

Askja Caldera

Askja Caldera is a prominent volcanic feature located in the northeastern region of Iceland. It is situated in the remote highlands of the country and forms part of the larger Vatnajökull National Park. Askja Caldera is renowned for its stunning beauty and geological significance.

The caldera itself is a vast depression that measures approximately 50 square kilometres (19 square miles) and was formed through a series of volcanic eruptions. It is believed that the initial formation of Askja Caldera occurred around 10,000 years ago during a massive volcanic event. Since then, the caldera has experienced several eruptions, with the most notable occurring in 1875 and 1961.

One of the most captivating features within the caldera is Öskjuvatn, a deep lake that formed within a smaller crater. Öskjuvatn is the deepest lake in Iceland, reaching depths of up to 220 metres (720 feet). The lake's mesmerising blue colour, set against the dramatic backdrop of the surrounding volcanic landscape, makes it a popular destination for visitors.

Askja Caldera and its surroundings offer a unique and otherworldly experience for adventurers and nature enthusiasts. The vast expanse of rugged lava fields, volcanic cones, and ash-covered landscapes provide a glimpse into Iceland's geological history. The area is also home to several volcanic fissures, hot springs, and geothermal areas, showcasing the intense geothermal activity of the region.

Despite its remote location and challenging accessibility, Askja Caldera attracts a significant number of visitors each year. Tourists can reach the caldera by travelling through the highlands via specialised tour vehicles, often accompanied by experienced guides. Hiking enthusiasts also have the option to embark on multi-day treks through the highlands to explore Askja and its surrounding volcanic wonders.

One of the most notable landmarks within the vicinity of Askja Caldera is the Víti crater. Víti, meaning "hell" in Icelandic, is a stunning volcanic crater filled with geothermal water. Visitors can often take a dip in its warm, mineral-rich waters, providing a truly unique bathing experience in the midst of a volcanic landscape.

It's worth noting that due to the remote location and potential hazards associated with volcanic activity, it's crucial for visitors to exercise caution and stay informed about any travel advisories or restrictions in the area. Additionally, proper planning, appropriate equipment, and adherence to safety guidelines are essential when exploring Askja Caldera and its surroundings.

Overall, Askja Caldera stands as a captivating testament to Iceland's volatile volcanic history. Its awe-inspiring landscapes, geological wonders, and secluded beauty make it a must-visit destination for those seeking an unforgettable adventure in Iceland's highlands.

Thorsmork Nature Reserve

Thorsmork Nature Reserve, also known as Þórsmörk, is a stunning wilderness area located in the southern highlands of Iceland. It is named after the Norse god Thor and is renowned for its breathtaking landscapes, rugged mountains, deep valleys, and glacial rivers. Thorsmork is a paradise for outdoor enthusiasts and nature lovers, offering a wide range of activities and stunning natural attractions.

Located between three glaciers—Mýrdalsjökull, Eyjafjallajökull, and Tindfjallajökull—Thorsmork provides a unique and diverse environment. The combination of glaciers, volcanoes, and rivers has carved out a magnificent and picturesque landscape. The area is covered in lush green vegetation, mossy forests, and colorful wildflowers during the summer months, creating a magical atmosphere.

One of the most popular activities in Thorsmork is hiking. The nature reserve offers numerous hiking trails, varying in difficulty and length, catering to both experienced hikers and beginners. The famous Laugavegur Trek, a multi-day hike, starts or finishes in Thorsmork, taking adventurers through awe-inspiring landscapes, hot springs, and volcanic valleys.

The Fimmvörðuháls Pass is another iconic trail in Thorsmork, leading hikers between the Eyjafjallajökull and Mýrdalsjökull glaciers. This route offers breathtaking views of glaciers, lava fields, and majestic waterfalls, including the famous Skógafoss and Seljalandsfoss.

Thorsmork is also a great place for camping, with designated campsites available for visitors. Spending a night under the starry sky in the midst of the pristine Icelandic wilderness is an unforgettable experience.

Aside from hiking and camping, Thorsmork offers opportunities for glacier tours, jeep safaris, and river crossing adventures. Visitors can explore the glacial rivers and witness the raw power of nature as they traverse the challenging terrain.

It's important to note that Thorsmork is a remote area with limited facilities, and proper preparation is essential. It is recommended to check weather conditions, carry appropriate gear, and be aware of potential hazards such as sudden changes in weather or river crossings. Local tour operators and guides can provide valuable assistance and ensure a safe and enjoyable experience.

Thorsmork Nature Reserve in Iceland is a true gem, providing visitors with an extraordinary opportunity to immerse themselves in the raw and untouched beauty of Iceland's highlands. Its unique blend of glacial and volcanic features, coupled with a sense of tranquillity and isolation, makes it a must-visit destination for nature enthusiasts seeking an unforgettable adventure.

Vestmannaeyjar Archipelago

Vestmannaeyjar, also known as the Westman Islands, is a picturesque archipelago situated off the south coast of Iceland. It consists of around fifteen islands and islets, with the largest and only inhabited island being Heimaey. Vestmannaeyjar is renowned for its stunning natural beauty, rich wildlife, and fascinating volcanic history.

The archipelago was formed by volcanic activity, and its most famous landmark is Eldfell, a volcanic cone that emerged during a volcanic eruption in 1973. This eruption had a significant impact on the island and its inhabitants, as they were forced to evacuate and a large part of the town was buried under lava. However, the islanders demonstrated resilience and determination by returning and rebuilding their homes, and the eruption ultimately created new land and added to the unique geological features of Vestmannaeyjar.

Vestmannaeyjar boasts diverse and abundant birdlife, with several species nesting in the cliffs and rocky shores of the islands. Puffins, in particular, are a major attraction, and visitors have the opportunity to observe these charming seabirds up close during the breeding season. The islands are also home to other seabirds, such as guillemots, razorbills, and kittiwakes.

The archipelago's marine environment is teeming with life, making it a popular destination for fishing and whale watching. Various species of whales, including orcas and humpbacks, can often be spotted in the surrounding waters. Visitors can embark on boat tours to experience these majestic creatures in their natural habitat.

In addition to its natural wonders, Vestmannaeyjar offers a range of outdoor activities. Hiking enthusiasts can explore the rugged landscapes and enjoy breathtaking views from the island's peaks, such as the Eldfell volcano. There are also opportunities for camping, golfing, and even swimming in the island's geothermally heated pools.

The town of Vestmannaeyjar on Heimaey Island serves as the archipelago's main hub. It has a charming harbour and offers amenities for visitors, including accommodations, restaurants, and museums. The Eldheimar Museum provides insights into the 1973 eruption and its impact on the community, while the Sagnheimar Museum focuses on the history and culture of the islands.

Reaching Vestmannaeyjar usually involves taking a ferry or a short flight from the Icelandic mainland. The archipelago's unique combination of volcanic landscapes, abundant wildlife, and resilient community make it a captivating destination for nature lovers and those seeking an off-the-beaten-path experience in Iceland.

CHAPTER 11. Practical Tips and Advice

Safety and Health Information

Safety and health information in Iceland focuses on ensuring the well-being of its residents and visitors. The country places a strong emphasis on promoting safety standards and providing reliable information to prevent accidents, injuries, and illnesses. Here are some key aspects of safety and health information in Iceland:

1. Occupational Health and Safety: Iceland has robust regulations and frameworks in place to protect workers' health and safety. The Administration of Occupational Safety and Health (AOSH) is responsible for enforcing these regulations and ensuring compliance in workplaces across the country. AOSH conducts inspections, provides training, and promotes awareness campaigns to minimise workplace hazards and promote safe working conditions.

2. Healthcare System: Iceland boasts a comprehensive healthcare system that offers high-quality medical services to its residents. The

healthcare system in Iceland is publicly funded and provides universal coverage, ensuring that everyone has access to necessary healthcare services. This includes preventive care, emergency services, and treatment for various health conditions.

3. Emergency Services: Iceland has well-developed emergency services to respond to various safety and health incidents. The Icelandic Association for Search and Rescue (ICE-SAR) plays a crucial role in search and rescue operations, particularly in remote and hazardous areas. They work closely with the Icelandic Coast Guard, police, and healthcare services to provide rapid and effective assistance during emergencies.

4. Road Safety: Iceland prioritises road safety and provides extensive information to ensure safe driving practices. The Icelandic Transport Authority (ITA) oversees road safety regulations and promotes initiatives aimed at reducing accidents. Visitors are encouraged to familiarize themselves with local driving laws, including speed limits, seatbelt usage, and driving conditions, which can vary due to Iceland's unique geography and weather.

5. Tourism Safety: Given Iceland's popularity as a tourist destination, safety information for travelers is readily available. The Icelandic Tourist Board offers guidelines and safety tips to ensure a positive and safe experience for visitors. These guidelines cover topics such as weather conditions, outdoor activities, water safety, and responsible tourism practices.

6. Public Health Alerts: In times of health emergencies or outbreaks, the Icelandic health authorities provide regular updates and public health alerts. The Directorate of Health (Landlæknisembættið) and the Chief Epidemiologist issue guidelines and recommendations to safeguard public health. These updates are disseminated through various channels, including websites, social media, and news outlets, to keep the public informed and provide necessary instructions.

It's important to note that safety and health information can evolve, and it's advisable to consult official sources, such as government websites and local authorities, for the most up-to-date and accurate information in Iceland.

Money and Currency Exchange

Iceland has a unique financial system and currency exchange regulations that are worth discussing. The official currency of Iceland is the Icelandic Króna (ISK). Here's some information about money and currency exchange in Iceland:

1. Icelandic Króna (ISK): The Icelandic Króna is the official currency of Iceland. The currency symbol for the Króna is "kr" or "ISK." Banknotes are available in denominations of 500 kr, 1,000 kr, 2,000 kr, 5,000 kr, and 10,000 kr. Coins are available in denominations of 1 kr, 5 kr, 10 kr, 50 kr, and 100 kr.

2. Currency Exchange: Currency exchange services are available at banks, exchange offices, and some hotels in Iceland. The exchange rates may vary, and it's advisable to compare rates to get the best deal. It's also worth noting that some banks might charge a commission or service fee for currency exchange.

3. Credit Cards: Credit cards are widely accepted in Iceland, and you can use them for most purchases and transactions. Major credit cards such as Visa and Mastercard are commonly used. However, it's always a good idea to carry some cash for small

purchases and in case you encounter a place that doesn't accept cards.

4. ATMs: ATMs (Automated Teller Machines) are available throughout Iceland, and they provide a convenient way to withdraw cash in the local currency. ATMs are typically found in cities, towns, and popular tourist areas. It's important to check with your bank regarding any international withdrawal fees or restrictions that may apply.

5. Currency Restrictions: Iceland has some currency restrictions in place. When entering or leaving the country, you must declare if you are carrying more than 10,000 euros or its equivalent in another currency. This declaration is necessary to prevent money laundering and illegal activities.

6. Foreign Currency Exchange: It's advisable to exchange your currency for Icelandic Króna once you arrive in Iceland. While some places may accept foreign currency, it's not as common, and you might receive change in local currency. Exchange rates for foreign currencies are generally less favorable outside of Iceland.

7. Price Levels: It's important to note that Iceland has a relatively high cost of living compared to

many other countries. Prices for goods and services, including accommodation, dining out, and transportation, can be higher than what you might be accustomed to. It's essential to budget accordingly and be prepared for the expenses.

As currency exchange rates and regulations can change over time, it's recommended to check with official sources or consult your bank for the most up-to-date information before travelling to Iceland.

Communication and Internet Access

Iceland is renowned for its advanced communication infrastructure and high internet penetration rates, making it one of the most connected countries in the world. The nation has invested heavily in telecommunications and internet technologies, resulting in widespread access to high-speed internet and reliable communication services.

Internet access in Iceland is widely available, with a high percentage of the population having access to broadband connections. The country has an extensive fibre optic network that spans across much of its territory, enabling fast and reliable internet connectivity. This infrastructure supports various internet service providers (ISPs) offering a range of packages to cater to different needs, from residential users to businesses.

The Icelandic government has taken significant steps to promote internet accessibility and digital literacy. They have implemented initiatives to ensure that even remote and rural areas have access to broadband services. This commitment to inclusivity has resulted in a high level of internet penetration, with a large percentage of the population enjoying internet connectivity.

Mobile communication is also highly developed in Iceland. The country has a well-established cellular network, providing excellent coverage throughout the country, including rural areas. Icelandic consumers have access to a range of mobile operators, offering competitive plans and services. Mobile data services are widely used, and the country has adopted advanced wireless technologies like 4G and 5G to cater to the increasing demand for high-speed mobile connectivity.

In terms of internet speed, Iceland ranks among the top countries globally. The average internet connection speed in the country is notably high, allowing for seamless streaming, online gaming, and other data-intensive activities. This fast internet speed has contributed to the growth of technology-driven industries, such as software development, gaming, and digital services.

Iceland is also known for its commitment to digital privacy and data protection. The country has robust regulations in place to safeguard user data and ensure privacy. Iceland's legal framework aligns with the European Union's General Data Protection Regulation (GDPR), providing individuals with control over their personal information.

In conclusion, Iceland boasts advanced communication infrastructure and widespread internet access. With a focus on inclusivity, the country has achieved high levels of internet penetration and offers fast and reliable internet connectivity. Icelanders enjoy excellent mobile coverage and benefit from a strong commitment to digital privacy. These factors have contributed to Iceland's reputation as a technologically advanced and well-connected nation.

Packing Essentials

When packing for a trip to Iceland, it's important to consider the unique climate and natural surroundings of the country. Here are some packing essentials to ensure you're prepared for your adventure:

1. Clothing layers: Iceland's weather can be unpredictable, so it's crucial to pack clothing that can be layered for warmth. Include thermal base layers, insulating mid-layers, and waterproof outer layers. Don't forget to pack a warm hat, gloves, and a scarf for added protection.

2. Waterproof and windproof gear: Iceland is known for its rain, wind, and ever-changing weather conditions. Pack a sturdy, waterproof jacket and pants to keep you dry during outdoor activities. A windproof layer is also recommended to shield you from the chilly winds.

3. Sturdy footwear: Exploring Iceland often involves walking on various terrains, including rocky landscapes, glaciers, and volcanic areas. Pack comfortable, waterproof hiking boots with good traction for your outdoor adventures. Also, consider bringing a pair of lightweight, quick-drying shoes or

sandals for relaxing moments or visits to hot springs.

4. Swimwear and towel: Iceland is famous for its geothermal pools, hot springs, and natural spas. Be sure to pack swimwear and a quick-drying towel so you can enjoy these unique experiences.

5. Travel adapter: Iceland uses the Europlug (Type C) and Schuko (Type F) electrical outlets. Make sure to bring a universal travel adapter to charge your electronic devices and keep them powered throughout your trip.

6. Medications and personal care items: If you require any prescription medications, be sure to pack an adequate supply. It's also advisable to carry a basic first aid kit, including pain relievers, band-aids, and any necessary personal care items.

7. Outdoor accessories: Don't forget to pack essential outdoor accessories such as a backpack, a reusable water bottle, a hat for sun protection, sunglasses, and sunscreen. These items will come in handy when you're exploring Iceland's breathtaking landscapes.

8. Camera equipment: Iceland offers incredible photo opportunities. If you enjoy photography, consider packing your camera gear, including spare batteries, memory cards, and a tripod, to capture the stunning landscapes and Northern Lights.

9. Travel documents: Remember to carry your passport, travel insurance documents, and any necessary visas. It's also a good idea to keep digital or physical copies of your important documents in case of loss or emergency.

10. Snacks and water: While there are grocery stores and restaurants in Iceland, it's wise to carry some snacks and a refillable water bottle during your outdoor adventures to stay hydrated and keep your energy levels up.

Remember to check the weather forecast for the specific period of your trip to Iceland and adjust your packing accordingly. By considering these essentials, you'll be well-prepared to enjoy the unique beauty and experiences that Iceland has to offer.

Local Etiquette and Customs

Iceland, a Nordic island country located in the North Atlantic Ocean, has its own unique local etiquette and customs. Here are some aspects of Icelandic culture that you may find interesting:

1. Greetings: When meeting someone in Iceland, it is customary to greet them with a firm handshake and maintain eye contact. Icelandic people tend to address each other using first names, regardless of social status or age, as they have a relatively informal culture.

2. Punctuality: Icelandic people value punctuality and appreciate it when others are on time for appointments or social gatherings. Being late without a valid reason is considered disrespectful. It's advisable to arrive a few minutes early if you have a scheduled meeting.

3. Personal space: Icelanders generally value their personal space and prefer to keep a comfortable distance when conversing with others. It's important to respect this boundary and avoid standing too close or touching someone without their permission.

4. Tipping: Unlike some other countries, tipping is not expected or common in Iceland. Service charges are often included in the bill, and employees receive fair wages. However, if you feel that the service provided was exceptional, a small tip would still be appreciated.

5. Dining customs: When invited to someone's home for a meal, it's customary to arrive on time and remove your shoes at the entrance unless told otherwise. Wait to be seated, and it's polite to compliment the host on the food. Burping at the table is considered impolite, while leaving a small amount of food on your plate indicates that you are full.

6. Nature and environment: Icelanders have a deep appreciation for their stunning natural surroundings. It is essential to respect the environment by staying on designated paths, not littering, and following any guidelines or restrictions in protected areas.

7. Hot springs and swimming pools: Iceland is known for its geothermal hot springs and swimming pools. Before entering a public pool or hot spring, it is customary to shower without clothing and thoroughly wash yourself. Nudity in

communal showers and changing rooms is generally accepted and part of the local culture.

8. Socializing: Icelanders enjoy socializing and engaging in conversations. When engaging in a conversation, it's polite to listen attentively and show genuine interest. Interrupting others while they are speaking is considered impolite.

9. Alcohol consumption: Alcohol is legal and commonly consumed in Iceland, but excessive drinking or disruptive behavior is generally frowned upon. It's important to drink responsibly and be mindful of others.

10. Clothing: Iceland's weather can be unpredictable, so it's advisable to dress in layers and be prepared for changing conditions. Locals tend to dress casually but neat and tidy for most occasions.

It's worth noting that while these customs are generally observed in Iceland, individual preferences and practices may vary. Icelanders are known for their friendly and welcoming nature, so embracing their culture and customs will enhance your experience when visiting the country.

CHAPTER 12. Icelandic Cuisine and Local Delicacies

Traditional Icelandic Dishes

Traditional Icelandic cuisine reflects the country's unique geographic location and the cultural traditions of its people. With its abundance of fresh fish, seafood, lamb, and dairy products, Icelandic cuisine offers a variety of flavours and dishes that have been enjoyed for centuries. Let's explore some traditional Icelandic dishes:

1. Plokkfiskur: Plokkfiskur is a popular Icelandic comfort food made from boiled fish (usually cod or haddock) and potatoes, mashed together and seasoned with onions, herbs, and sometimes béchamel sauce. It's a hearty and flavorful dish often served with rye bread.

2. Hangikjöt: Hangikjöt is a traditional Icelandic smoked lamb dish. It is prepared by smoking the lamb over birch wood, which gives it a distinctive smoky flavour. The meat is typically sliced and served with boiled potatoes, white sauce, and peas.

It is a classic dish enjoyed during the Christmas season.

3. Harðfiskur: Harðfiskur is a dried fish snack commonly eaten in Iceland. It is made by air-drying fish, usually cod or haddock, until it becomes hard and crispy. Harðfiskur is often eaten as a snack or served with butter, especially when hiking or travelling.

4. Icelandic Lamb Soup: Icelandic Lamb Soup, known as kjötsúpa, is a traditional and comforting dish. It features tender lamb meat, potatoes, carrots, and onions, simmered in a flavorful broth until everything is tender and delicious. It's often served with homemade bread and butter.

5. Skyr: Skyr is a thick and creamy dairy product that resembles yoghourt but has a slightly different production process. It has been a staple of the Icelandic diet since the Viking era. Skyr is high in protein and low in fat, making it a healthy and popular choice for breakfast or as a snack. It can be enjoyed plain or with various toppings, such as berries, honey, or granola.

6. Kleinur: Kleinur are traditional Icelandic pastries that are similar to doughnuts or twisted

breadsticks. They are made from a sweet dough that is shaped into twisted rings and deep-fried until golden brown. Kleinur are often enjoyed with a cup of coffee or tea and are particularly popular during festive occasions.

7. Brennivín: While not a dish per se, Brennivín is a traditional Icelandic schnapps often referred to as "Black Death" due to its high alcohol content and strong flavour. It is distilled from fermented potato mash and flavoured with caraway seeds. Brennivín is commonly consumed during the mid-winter festival called Þorrablót and is sometimes served as a shot alongside traditional Icelandic dishes.

These are just a few examples of the traditional Icelandic dishes you can find in Iceland. The country's cuisine embraces the natural resources available and showcases the flavours and culinary heritage of the Icelandic people.

Seafood Specialties

Iceland is renowned for its pristine waters and abundant marine resources, making it a paradise for seafood lovers. The country's unique geographical location, with its cold North Atlantic Ocean surrounding the island, provides an ideal environment for a wide variety of seafood. Here are some seafood specialties you can enjoy in Iceland:

1. Icelandic Langoustine: Langoustine, also known as Icelandic lobster, is a delicacy that takes centre stage in Icelandic cuisine. These succulent crustaceans are usually boiled or grilled and served with melted butter, garlic, and various herbs. The langoustine's sweet and tender meat is highly sought after by locals and visitors alike.

2. Icelandic Salmon: Iceland is home to some of the world's best salmon fishing grounds. Icelandic salmon is known for its exceptional quality and flavour. Whether enjoyed smoked, grilled, or baked, the salmon's rich and buttery texture is a true delight.

3. Arctic Char: This cold-water fish is closely related to salmon and trout, and it thrives in Iceland's pristine rivers and lakes. Arctic char has delicate pink flesh with a slightly milder flavour than salmon. It can be prepared in numerous ways, such as pan-frying, grilling, or oven-baking, and is often served with flavorful sauces or citrus-based marinades.

4. Icelandic Cod: Cod holds a special place in Icelandic cuisine and has been a staple for centuries. Icelandic cod is renowned for its firm, white flesh and mild flavour. It is commonly enjoyed in dishes like traditional fish and chips, as well as in more sophisticated preparations such as pan-seared cod fillets with herb-infused butter.

5. Icelandic Haddock: Haddock is another popular fish found in Icelandic waters. It has a delicate, slightly sweet flavour and tender flesh. Haddock is commonly used in classic Icelandic dishes like plokkfiskur, a creamy fish stew made with potatoes, onions, and various seasonings.

6. Icelandic Mussels: Icelandic mussels are known for their exceptional quality and flavour. They are often harvested along the country's coastlines and served in dishes like moules marinières, where they are cooked with white wine, garlic, and herbs. The mussels' briny taste and plump texture make them a true delight for seafood enthusiasts.

7. Icelandic Scallops: Scallops are prized for their delicate flavour and tender texture. Icelandic scallops are no exception, offering a sweet and succulent taste. They are commonly seared or

grilled to bring out their natural sweetness and served as an appetiser or main course.

When visiting Iceland, be sure to explore the local seafood restaurants, where you can indulge in these exquisite seafood specialties and experience the freshness and natural flavours that make Icelandic seafood so exceptional.

Unique Ingredients and Flavours

Iceland is known for its stunning landscapes and vibrant culture, but it also has a unique culinary scene with a range of ingredients and flavours that reflect its natural resources and traditions. Here are some unique ingredients and flavours you can find in Icelandic cuisine:

1. Icelandic Lamb: Iceland's lamb is renowned for its exceptional flavor. The sheep roam freely in the country's unspoiled landscapes, feeding on wild herbs and grasses, resulting in tender and flavorful meat. Lamb dishes like smoked lamb, lamb stew (kjötsúpa), and lamb chops are popular in Iceland.

2. Skyr: Skyr is a traditional Icelandic dairy product that resembles yogurt but has a thicker and creamier texture. It has been a part of Icelandic

cuisine for centuries and is made from skim milk. Skyr is high in protein and low in fat, making it a healthy and popular choice for breakfast or a snack. It is often served with berries, honey, or granola.

3. Icelandic Fish: With its extensive coastline and abundant fishing grounds, Iceland is known for its high-quality seafood. Common fish varieties include cod, haddock, salmon, trout, and Arctic char. Icelandic fish is often prepared using simple cooking techniques to highlight the natural flavors. Popular dishes include traditional fish stew (plokkfiskur) and pan-fried fish.

4. Rúgbrauð (Icelandic Rye Bread): Rúgbrauð is a traditional Icelandic rye bread that is dense, moist, and slightly sweet. It is baked slowly in geothermal ovens buried in the ground, giving it a distinct flavor. Rúgbrauð is often served with butter, smoked fish, or gravlax.

5. Brennivín: Brennivín is a traditional Icelandic schnapps made from fermented potatoes and flavored with caraway seeds. It is often referred to as "Black Death" due to its high alcohol content and strong taste. Brennivín is typically enjoyed as a shot, and it is sometimes served alongside

fermented shark (hákarl) for a traditional Icelandic pairing.

6. Arctic Berries: Iceland is home to a variety of wild berries that thrive in the country's unique climate. These include crowberries, blueberries, bilberries, and wild strawberries. Arctic berries are rich in flavor and often used in desserts, jams, and sauces.

7. Moss: Iceland's volcanic landscape is covered in vibrant green moss, and it has found its way into the country's cuisine. Moss is harvested and used in traditional dishes such as moss soup and moss-covered lamb. It adds a unique earthy flavor and texture to these dishes.

8. Sea Vegetables: Iceland's coastal waters offer an abundance of sea vegetables, including kelp, dulse, and seaweed. These ingredients are gaining popularity for their umami-rich flavors and nutritional benefits. Sea vegetables are often used in salads, soups, and as a garnish for seafood dishes.

Iceland's cuisine celebrates its natural resources, from the high-quality lamb and seafood to unique ingredients like skyr, rúgbrauð, and Arctic berries.

Exploring the flavors of Iceland can be a delightful experience for food enthusiasts and those seeking to experience the country's culinary traditions.

Recommended Restaurants and Cafes

Iceland offers a unique culinary experience, blending traditional Icelandic cuisine with international influences. From cozy cafes to fine dining establishments, here are some recommended restaurants and cafes in Iceland:

1. Dill (Reykjavik): Dill is a renowned Michelin-starred restaurant in Reykjavik, known for its emphasis on locally sourced and foraged ingredients. They offer a seasonal tasting menu that showcases the best of Icelandic flavors and innovative techniques.

2. Kolabrautin (Reykjavik): Located on the top floor of the Harpa Concert Hall, Kolabrautin offers panoramic views of Reykjavik's skyline. The menu features a fusion of Icelandic and Mediterranean cuisine, with dishes like lamb fillet and langoustine.

3. Fiskmarkaðurinn (Reykjavik): Also known as The Fish Market, this restaurant focuses on seafood and Icelandic delicacies. Their menu includes dishes like Arctic char, langoustine soup, and grilled Icelandic lobster, prepared with a modern twist.

4. Grillmarkaðurinn (Reykjavik): Situated in a historic building in downtown Reykjavik, Grillmarkaðurinn, or The Grill Market, combines traditional Icelandic ingredients with contemporary cooking methods. The menu features grilled meats, local fish, and seasonal vegetables.

5. Matur og Drykkur (Reykjavik): Matur og Drykkur celebrates Icelandic culinary heritage by reviving traditional recipes with a modern touch. They use locally sourced ingredients to create dishes such as cured salmon, reindeer, and fermented shark.

6. Slippbarinn (Reykjavik): Located in the trendy Marina Hotel, Slippbarinn is a popular bar and restaurant offering a vibrant atmosphere. They serve a variety of dishes, including burgers, fish and chips, and vegetarian options, accompanied by creative cocktails.

7. Fridheimar (Selfoss): Located in a greenhouse in the Golden Circle region, Fridheimar specializes in

dishes made with tomatoes grown on-site. You can enjoy tomato-based soups, pasta, and even tomato-themed desserts in this unique setting.

8. Kaffi Loki (Reykjavik): For a taste of traditional Icelandic treats, visit Kaffi Loki. They serve traditional dishes such as Icelandic rye bread, smoked lamb, and fermented shark. Don't miss the opportunity to try their popular rye bread ice cream.

9. Cafe Paris (Reykjavik): This charming cafe captures the essence of a European-style coffeehouse. You can indulge in a selection of pastries, cakes, and sandwiches while enjoying the cozy ambiance and people-watching in downtown Reykjavik.

10. Cafe Babalú (Akureyri): If you find yourself in the northern town of Akureyri, make sure to visit Cafe Babalú. This cozy cafe is known for its excellent coffee, homemade cakes, and sandwiches. It's the perfect spot to relax after exploring the beautiful surroundings.

These are just a few of the many wonderful restaurants and cafes you can explore in Iceland. Whether you're seeking traditional Icelandic cuisine or international flavours, you're sure to find a delightful dining experience to suit your tastes.

CHAPTER 13. Language and Useful Phrases

Basic Icelandic Phrases

Here are some basic Icelandic phrases that can be useful when visiting Iceland:

1. Góðan daginn (Good day) - This is a common greeting used throughout the day.

2. Bless (Goodbye) - Use this phrase when saying goodbye to someone.

3. Já (Yes) - Use this word to express agreement or affirmation.

4. Nei (No) - This word is used to express disagreement or negation.

5. Takk (Thank you) - Use this phrase to express gratitude or appreciation.

6. Vinsamlegast (Please) - Use this word to make a polite request or to add politeness to a sentence.

7. Hvar er...? (Where is...?) - You can use this phrase to ask for directions to a specific place or location. For example, "Hvar er sundlaugin?" means "Where is the swimming pool?"

8. Ég skil ekki (I don't understand) - Use this phrase when you don't understand something and need clarification.

9. Ég tala ekki íslensku (I don't speak Icelandic) - If you don't speak Icelandic, you can use this phrase to let people know that you don't understand the language.

10. Hvað kostar þetta? (How much does this cost?) - Use this phrase when you want to know the price of something.

Remember, Icelanders generally speak English fluently, especially in tourist areas. However, making an effort to learn a few basic Icelandic phrases can be appreciated by the locals and enhance your travel experience in Iceland.

English Proficiency in Iceland

English proficiency in Iceland is quite high, with a large portion of the population being proficient in the English language. English is taught as a compulsory subject in schools from a young age, and many Icelanders continue to use and improve their English skills throughout their lives.

The high level of English proficiency in Iceland can be attributed to several factors. Firstly, Iceland has a small population and a highly educated society, which allows for more focused attention on language education. English is considered an important skill for Icelanders due to the country's reliance on tourism and international trade.

Furthermore, Icelandic television programs and movies are often subtitled rather than dubbed, which exposes Icelanders to the English language from an early age. This exposure to English media helps develop listening and comprehension skills.

Additionally, Icelanders are known for their proficiency in languages in general. Many Icelanders are bilingual or even multilingual, with English being one of the most common languages spoken alongside Icelandic. This multilingualism is encouraged through language exchange programs and opportunities to study abroad.

English proficiency in Iceland is particularly strong among younger generations, as English is becoming increasingly prevalent in popular culture and digital media. Young Icelanders are often fluent in English and are comfortable using it in various contexts, including social media, online communication, and academic settings.

Overall, the English proficiency in Iceland is impressive, with a large portion of the population being able to communicate effectively in English. This proficiency is a result of strong language education, exposure to English media, and a culture that values multilingualism.

Language Learning Resources

Language learning resources in Iceland can be diverse and tailored to suit various learning styles and preferences. Icelanders are known for their proficiency in English, but if you're interested in learning the Icelandic language, there are several resources available to assist you. Here are some popular language learning resources in Iceland:

1. Icelandic Language Courses: Numerous language schools and institutions offer Icelandic language courses in Iceland. These courses cater to both

beginners and advanced learners and usually cover various aspects of the language, including grammar, vocabulary, pronunciation, and conversation skills.

2. Online Learning Platforms: With the rise of online education, there are numerous websites and platforms that offer Icelandic language courses and study materials. Websites like Icelandic Online (Icelandic Online: Learn Icelandic! (icelandiconline.is)) provide interactive lessons, exercises, and resources to help learners practice and improve their language skills.

3. Mobile Apps: Language learning apps have gained immense popularity due to their convenience and accessibility. Apps like Memrise, Drops, and Duolingo offer Icelandic language courses and vocabulary-building exercises. These apps usually provide gamified learning experiences to make the process more engaging and enjoyable.

4. Books and Textbooks: You can find various Icelandic language learning books and textbooks that cater to different proficiency levels. These resources typically cover grammar rules, vocabulary, reading exercises, and cultural insights. Additionally, some books may include audio materials or CDs to help with pronunciation.

5. Language Exchange Groups: Joining language exchange groups or language meetups in Iceland can be a valuable resource for language learners. These groups provide opportunities to practice speaking Icelandic with native speakers, get feedback, and engage in language-related activities. Websites like Meetup.com and Facebook groups often list language exchange events and gatherings in Iceland.

6. Online Language Forums and Communities: Joining online language learning forums and communities focused on Icelandic can be beneficial. Websites like Reddit and language learning forums have dedicated sections where learners can ask questions, seek advice, and connect with fellow learners and native speakers.

7. Icelandic Language Websites and Media: Exploring Icelandic language websites, newspapers, books, and other media can help learners immerse themselves in the language. Websites like Vísir (visir.is) and RÚV (ruv.is) offer news, articles, and other content in Icelandic. Reading and listening to Icelandic media can aid in improving vocabulary and comprehension skills.

8. Language Learning Podcasts: Podcasts specifically designed for language learners can be a great resource for practising listening skills. "Icelandic Online" offers a podcast series that focuses on various aspects of the Icelandic language, providing learners with dialogues, explanations, and exercises.

Remember, while these resources can be valuable, consistent practice, dedication, and immersion are key to effectively learning a new language. Additionally, engaging with native speakers and seeking opportunities to apply your skills in real-life situations will greatly enhance your language learning journey.

CHAPTER 14. Additional Resources

Recommended Books and Travel Guides

Iceland, with its stunning landscapes, rich history, and unique culture, is a fascinating destination for travellers. Whether you're planning a trip to Iceland or simply interested in learning more about the country, there are several recommended books and travel guides that can enhance your understanding and enjoyment of this beautiful Nordic island. Here are a few suggestions:

1. "The Little Book of Tourists in Iceland: Tips, Tricks, and What the Icelanders Really Think of You" by Alda Sigmundsdóttir: This insightful and humorous guidebook provides valuable tips for travelers visiting Iceland. It offers practical advice on navigating the local customs, understanding Icelandic culture, and getting the most out of your trip. It's a great read for those seeking a blend of practical information and entertaining anecdotes.

2. "The Sagas of Icelanders" edited by Örnólfur Thorsson: Iceland's sagas are a collection of

captivating mediaeval narratives that offer a glimpse into the country's history and mythology. This book brings together some of the most famous sagas, providing a fascinating exploration of Viking-age Iceland. It's an excellent choice for readers interested in Icelandic folklore and the country's literary heritage.

3. "Names for the Sea: Strangers in Iceland" by Sarah Moss: This memoir recounts the experiences of an Englishwoman living in Iceland with her family. Moss offers an intimate portrayal of Icelandic life, describing the challenges and joys of adapting to a new culture. It's a beautifully written book that provides a personal perspective on the country and its people.

4. "Iceland's Bell" by Halldór Laxness: Halldór Laxness, the Nobel Prize-winning Icelandic author, is renowned for his literary contributions. "Iceland's Bell" is a historical novel set in 18th-century Iceland, delving into the country's struggles for independence and the lives of its people. Laxness' writing style captures the essence of Icelandic society and landscapes, making it a must-read for literature enthusiasts.

5. "Lonely Planet Iceland" by Lonely Planet: As a trusted travel guide publisher, Lonely Planet offers a comprehensive guidebook on Iceland. It covers everything from practical travel information, such as accommodation and transportation, to detailed insights into the country's attractions, including its natural wonders, historic sites, and cultural highlights. It's an invaluable resource for planning your trip and exploring Iceland's diverse regions.

These are just a few recommendations, and there are many other books and travel guides available that cater to different interests and preferences. Whether you're seeking practical travel advice or a deeper understanding of Icelandic culture and history, these resources can enrich your experience of exploring Iceland.

Online Travel

Online travel in Iceland has become increasingly popular in recent years, enabling travellers from around the world to explore and plan their trips to this stunning Nordic island. Iceland offers a unique travel experience with its breathtaking landscapes, geothermal wonders, vibrant culture, and adventurous activities. The internet has played a significant role in making Iceland more accessible and helping travellers make the most of their journeys.

One of the key aspects of online travel in Iceland is the ability to research and plan your trip in advance. Numerous travel websites, blogs, and forums provide a wealth of information about Iceland's attractions, accommodations, transportation options, and recommended itineraries. These online resources offer insights into popular destinations such as the Golden Circle, the Blue Lagoon, Reykjavik, the South Coast, and the stunning waterfalls and glaciers.

Booking accommodations and transportation has also been made convenient through online platforms. Travellers can explore a wide range of options, from luxury hotels to cosy guesthouses, traditional farm stays, and unique accommodations like geodesic domes or glass igloos for observing the Northern Lights. Many websites offer comprehensive booking services, allowing visitors to compare prices, read reviews, and secure their reservations with just a few clicks.

Additionally, online platforms provide an opportunity to book various tours and activities in Iceland. Whether you're interested in exploring ice caves, hiking on glaciers, snorkelling in Silfra, riding Icelandic horses, or chasing the elusive Northern Lights, you can find and book these experiences online in advance. This ensures that travellers can secure their spots and plan their itineraries accordingly.

Another important aspect of online travel in Iceland is the availability of virtual resources to enhance the travel experience. Travellers can access interactive maps, detailed guides, and travel apps that provide real-time information about road conditions, weather forecasts, and recommended stops along the way. These tools are particularly valuable when exploring Iceland's remote areas and planning self-drive adventures.

Furthermore, social media platforms have played a significant role in promoting Iceland as a travel destination. Influencers and travel enthusiasts share their experiences, photos, and videos online, inspiring others to visit Iceland and providing valuable tips and insights. Hashtags like #Iceland, #IcelandTravel, and #InspiredByIceland have become popular, creating a vibrant online community of Iceland enthusiasts.

However, while online travel has numerous benefits, it's essential to balance virtual exploration with on-the-ground experiences. Iceland's rugged landscapes and natural wonders are best appreciated in person. It's important for travellers to disconnect from technology at times and immerse themselves in the awe-inspiring beauty of the country.

In conclusion, online travel has revolutionised the way people explore and plan their trips to Iceland. It has made information easily accessible, streamlined booking processes, and connected travellers from around the world. Through online platforms, travellers can embark on virtual journeys, research accommodations and activities, and make informed decisions to ensure an unforgettable experience in Iceland.